WONDER VERSE

Treasures Of Imagination

Edited By Lynsey Evans

First published in Great Britain in 2025 by:

Young Writers Est. 1991

Young Writers
Remus House
Coltsfoot Drive
Peterborough
PE2 9BF
Telephone: 01733 890066
Website: www.youngwriters.co.uk

FOREWORD

WELCOME READER,

For Young Writers' latest competition *Wonderverse*, we asked primary school pupils to explore their creativity and write a poem on any topic that inspired them. They rose to the challenge magnificently with some going even further and writing stories too! The result is this fantastic collection of writing in a variety of styles.

Here at Young Writers our aim is to encourage creativity in children and to inspire a love of the written word, so it's great to get such an amazing response, with some absolutely fantastic pieces. This open theme of this competition allowed them to write freely about something they are interested in, which we know helps to engage kids and get them writing. Within these pages you'll find a variety of topics, from hopes, fears and dreams, to favourite things and worlds of imagination. The result is a collection of brilliant writing that showcases the creativity and writing ability of the next generation.

I'd like to congratulate all the young writers in this anthology, I hope this inspires them to continue with their creative writing.

CONTENTS

Harvey Robinson (9) 73
Elenore Cooke (9) 74
Matthew Compton (9) 75
Finley Jones (10) 76
Esme Evans (9) 77

Larkfield Primary School, Southport

Amber Perkins (8) 78
Redwana Shamsia (10) 79
Eleanor Wright (9) 80
Kai Goldring-Jones (9) 81
Caleigh Jones (9) 82
Oliver Haughton (10) 83
Matthew Stark (10) 84
Arabella Woods (7) 85
Noah Taylor (9) 86
Ryan Ogden (10) 87
Ethan Webster (10) 88
Declan Ejchart (10) 89
Connie Dempster (9) 90
Melissa Wright (9) 91

Mendlesham Primary School, Mendlesham

Elsie Brundell (9) 92
Isla Clements (10) 93
Edith Cornell (9) 94
Lucia Faliveno (8) 95
Harrison Clements (10) 96

Meole Brace Church Of England Primary And Nursery, Shrewsbury

Sophia Bywater (9) 97
Elliot Taylor (9) 98
Ayomide Dawodu (9) 100
Oliver Roughan (8) 101
Bess Dargan (8) 102
Marcus Macam (8) 103
Imogen Lancaster (8) 104
Kamica Edmunds (9) 105

Lydia Talbot (8) 106
Mason Pritchard-Evans (8) 107
Jack Shaw-Rawlings (9) 108
Sophie Edgerton (8) 109
Jesse Lee (8) 110
Louie McDowall (9) 111
Amira Gregory (8) 112
Sienna Evans (9) 113
Evie Walker (8) 114
Darcy Hustwayte (8) 115
Benjamin Harrison (8) 116
Finley Greer (9) 117
Jack Sanders (9) 118
Roman Oliver (8) 119
Merryn Baker (8) 120
Ayda Dawson (8) 121
Owen Mellor (9) 122
Juke Williams (9) 123
Lacey Seyffert (8) 124
Romy Hales (9) 125
Genevieve Tanner-Stokes (9) 126
Eli Burgoyne (8) 127
Joseph Warren (9) 128
Maria Annunziata (8) 129
Harper Beatty (8) 130
Izzy Kirby-Murray (8) 131
Beatrix Doughty (8) 132
Sandaru Abeywickrama (8) 133
Owen Cornwell (8) 134
Booker Pitas (8) 135
Adrian Yomens (9) 136
Dylan Harris (9) 137
Mason Davies (8) 138
Logan Chidlow (9) 139
Conor Thomas (9) 140
Aimee Cartwright (8) 141
Oscar Rutherford (8) 142
Lucy Butler (8) 143
Alba Evans (8) 144
Lottie Dee (8) 145
Lily Evans (8) 146

Portway Junior School, Allestree

Lucas Tartari Franceschini (10)	147
Imogen Marriott	148
Robyn Stevenson	150
Agnes Crowley (9)	151
Nora Watkinson (8)	152
Finn Waldron (9)	153
Phoenix Morgan (9)	154
Connie Newboult (9)	155
Ella Kelsall (9)	156
Keziah Beatham (9)	157
Isabelle Walker (10)	158
Emmy Gardner (9)	159
Brenee (10)	160
Ebony Carmichael (9)	161

St Eanswythe's CE Primary School, Folkestone

Pritisha Lahkar (10)	162
Vlad Lynnyk (10)	164
Aurora Portnyagin (9)	165
Alexander Wilkes (10)	166
Ruby Nice (10)	167

St Michael's CE (A) First School, Penkridge

Leo Charles (8)	168
Esmae Boreland (8)	170
Autumn Byrne (9)	171
Elsie Shearwood (9)	172
Jacoby Landsborough (8)	173
Deyan P (8)	174
Millie-Jane Ainsworth (9)	175
Olivia Withington (8)	176
Ivy Armitage (8)	177
Holly Wootton (9)	178

St Silas CE Primary School, Blackburn

Haadiya Saifullah (10)	179
Ummul Khair Jamil (7)	180

Anayah Ali (10)	181
Hira Ashraf (8)	182
Eleora Onuyoh-Adaitire (8)	184
Ermina Lokhandwalu (10)	185
Kiran Ilyas (8)	186
Azwa Saifullah (8)	187
Imaan Ahsan (10)	188
Khalifa Khalifa (9)	189
Myiesha Umair (9)	190
Ali Dudhara (8)	191

The Python Hill Academy, Rainworth

Harmony Whitehouse (10)	192
Kacie Olivia Jepson (10)	194
Georgia Cox (10)	195
Macey Green (10)	196
Evie-May Lebeter (10)	198
Skyla Pearce (10)	199
Katelin Jane Ross (9)	200
Ruby-Mae White (10)	201
Lily Hatcher (10)	202
Evie Dakin (10)	203
Abigail Newey (11)	204

Truro High School For Girls, Truro

Kara Prideaux-Brune (10)	205
Agnes Watkins (9)	206
Ashleigh Balsdon (10)	207
Cecilia Srikanthan (9)	208
Annabelle Cave (9)	209
Olivia Chapman (10)	210
Charlotte Fox (9)	211
Matilda Soar (9)	212
Georgie Hose (9)	213
Sienna Hensher (9)	214
Dora Galsworthy (9)	215
Beany Sautelle-Smith (9)	216
Indie Singer (10)	217
Florence Floyd (9)	218
Nia Burnard (9)	219
Grace Hamilton (9)	220

Lula Myers (9)	221
Flo Latham (9)	222
Lily Eustice (9)	223
Maisie Green (9)	224

Woodcote House School, Windlesham

Rafe Mitchell (10)	225
Charlie Brittain (11)	226
Kevin Liu (10)	227
Daniel Bore (11)	228
Henry Stephenson (10)	229
Hans Matharu (10)	230
Inigo Worth (11)	231
Herbie Martin (10)	232
Alex Chase (10)	233
Ralph Gutu (11)	234
Casper Wyke (10)	235
Jonny Palmer (10)	236
Jaime Venero Loyo (10)	237

THE
CREATIVE
WRITING

The Child

"I lay on the ground covered in mud in the mossy landscape in between two mountainous trees in the east of Brazil with hardly any food or water."
He had just a little food and water
He had just a little food and water
He had just a little food and water
"In a rainforest whenever I get water I always give it to the plants, and as a result I do not get enough water."
He doesn't get enough water
He doesn't get enough water
He doesn't get enough water
"To get more water I made a pipe that transfers the water to my den."
He made a pipe
He made a pipe that transfers water to his den
He made a pipe
"To get my food I grab fish and let them suffocate. This is a day in the life of me, a child, a survivor."

George Dell'Osa (9)
Grand Avenue Primary And Nursery School, Surbiton

Infinite Void

In the hollowness of the dark, gloomy night,
You'll hear blood all over the ground, it quietly rots,
The marvellous, milky moonlight illuminates rocks,
That are blanketed in blood clots,
Reflecting what darkness is trying to hide.

What is this place... Who knows?

Vampires showing their venomous, terrifying teeth,
As they cackle with a haunting melody on the ground
beneath,
The trees trembling as the wind passes by,
While the vampires transform into a bat so they can
fly,
They fly and glide, high in the sky,
Their wings dark like a black hole,
As darkness grips from behind,
Prolonging the span of the endless night.

Their fangs have taken lives of countless poor souls,
As it pierces through the soft skin,
A splash of blood stains the fangs,
Next to it sits a skull once full of memories
Now empty and hollow
All that's left are the dead bodies that lie deep in the
forest

With their bones rotting on the ground
The vampires grimacing and wiping the blood off their
gruesome gnarled nails

The forest is haunted by what's left behind
Bones of humans and creatures unknown
The trees sigh, witnessing the traumatic sight in the
night
There's no place to hide
Vampires crave precious blood and always leave the
cold body behind

Where is this place? Who knows...?

Junaid Chowdhary (9)
Grand Avenue Primary And Nursery School, Surbiton

Women's Football Heroes

Sam Kerr
Australia's Sam Kerr
As she's speeding down the pitch like a blur
Sam
Bam! Wham!
Into the goal
Celebrating with her fam
She is Sam Kerr
And she will purr.

Lucy Bronze
England's Lucy Bronze
As she watches the opposition flee
Eating them up, one, two, three!
One look, then she's gone
Game on, she's won!

Millie Bright
Millie Bright
Is England's light
Trying to defend the goal with all her might
Millie Bright
Is a star in the night
Shining so bright

While giving a little fright
Running as fast as light.

Gabby Dunn (9)

Grand Avenue Primary And Nursery School, Surbiton

Friendship Is Forever

Friendship is forever
If you make a friend, it will stay like that forever
Having my best friend right by my side
Is something you can cherish in your life

Friendship is forever
Make a friend and let them stay in your life
Make new friends as well though
To try new things

Friendship is forever
Always try to make new friends
Friends are the key to your world
Friends are the key to your life

Friendship is forever
Use your friendship as a key to help people
Use your friendship as a key to be a kind friend
Use your friendship as a key to be courageous.

Olivia Georgiou (9)
Grand Avenue Primary And Nursery School, Surbiton

Space

We are the planets of the universe
Where do we live?
Space
Outstanding outer space
It is blue
Navy blue
Royal, Cambridge even
Sapphire
Endless possibilities
Go into space
And explore
Uncover what is hidden
Deep inside space
It is a vacuum
Nearly void of matter
And with extremely low pressure
The astronauts who see
Astonishing space
Are amazed by the vastness
And beautifulness of space
Place your hand into mine
And drift into space.

Sadie Kelliher Davies (9)
Grand Avenue Primary And Nursery School, Surbiton

7

The Beast Within Me!

I hid within me so as not to be seen
Forever this has been.

I didn't shed a tear out of fear
But waited to be safe at home and alone
To let the beast of sadness roam.

Listened to and heard made me feel open and ready
To accept the challenge for change.

I faced my fear and grew bigger within
Danced and smiled, despite the fight and what had
been.

It took time for me to shine and to rise up
Finally free and filled with glee
I am able to be me.

Amelie Habes (9)
Grand Avenue Primary And Nursery School, Surbiton

I Am...

I am the soul of the waterfall,
The heart of the sea,
The beauty of the dolphins,
They all lead back to me.
My given gift of glory thrives,
Between my bones,
And if you look at me closely,
You will see my many tones.

I am the mother of the spark of your love and romance,
With a glimpse of something dangerous... so, be
careful.

I am the streams of light flowing through your window
in the early months.
In spring I bring colour to the buttercups and daisies.

Mia Johnson (10)
Grand Avenue Primary And Nursery School, Surbiton

The Girl Who Loved Nature!

Nature is my happy place,
It makes me feel calm.
It is my freedom.
If I climb a tree,
I feel alive.
I see the honey-coloured autumn leaves falling in midair,
Watching flowers shed their petals onto the frosty grass.

Nature is my happy place,
It makes me feel alive.
The smell of freshly cut grass
And animals making their way back home.
Watching the fiery shades painting pictures in the sky.

Nature is my happy place!

Raffy Thompson (9)
Grand Avenue Primary And Nursery School, Surbiton

Green

"Use me," said green
"I am eco-friendly
I love broccoli and sprouts
My lush grass blows in the wind
It is always wheat and neat
I am the colour of plants."

In my world, everything is
Green, green, green, green.
My colour has beauty
From emeralds to dark green
I am the shade of leaves
On the trees
I am the best
On top of the rest
Because my colour is the best.

Leah Jones (9)
Grand Avenue Primary And Nursery School, Surbiton

Which Pet?

A dog may bite
A cat may scratch
And I certainly do not want a rat.

Rabbits are cool
Hamsters squeak
Chinchillas have very long teeth.

Birds are colourful
Spiders are scary
And fish are too slimy.

Rottweilers are too big
Mice are too small
And snakes are too long.

I have made my decision.
I am getting all of them!

Eidie Trimmer (9)
Grand Avenue Primary And Nursery School, Surbiton

Insects

I n a precious garden lies a group of mysterious creatures

N ow, they are pollinating nectar from a flower

S hall they complete it, yes or no?

E co-friendly animals are always ablaze

C ute creatures from the swirly type to the flying type

T hey all make an impact on our amazing lives

S o, be kind and make an insect hotel.

Artin Eilami (9)
Grand Avenue Primary And Nursery School, Surbiton

Fish

Fish swim as the water comes and goes
Fish discover a new land underwater
Fish swim in water as clear as crystal
My fish are green, orange and different shades of blue
My fish, some die, some live, but still remembered
My fish are swimming and roaming their tank
Fish are all remembered and are all loved by me and you.

Jackson Wright (9)
Grand Avenue Primary And Nursery School, Surbiton

Guinea Pig

Guinea pigs like to play hide-and-seek
And squeak and eat
And they like to munch on curly kale
And crunchy carrots.

They like to run around
And are fun to play with
Guinea pigs can be fluffy scruffy
Their fur can be long
Short or curly.

My guinea pigs are my best friends.

Zoe Ingram (10)
Grand Avenue Primary And Nursery School, Surbiton

Reading

Reading, oh gosh, it causes bleeding
Reading, I hate it, anything greater
Reading, such long pages; it takes ages

Reading is never pleading
Reading sometimes it's needing
Reading you never concentrate
While trying to finish your plate
Reading, *I just hate it!*

Oscar Selby (10)
Grand Avenue Primary And Nursery School, Surbiton

Muddy Paws

Muddy paws, rough and tumble,
Through the trees, like a jungle.

A wagging tail that never ends,
Tells me we are the best of friends.

Muddy paws, a sign of fun,
Time to chill out in the sun.

Fur so soft like a teddy bear,
Cuddles and love are always there.

Harriet Loxton (9)
Grand Avenue Primary And Nursery School, Surbiton

Autumn Is Here

Autumn is breezy, with the orange leaves rustling everywhere.
Umbrellas are out, for the long showers.
Time is ticking for me and you, look at the trees, golden brown.
Up in the trees, all you can see is brown and breeze.
Making magnificent memories in the season.

Jaanvi Patel (9)
Grand Avenue Primary And Nursery School, Surbiton

Sahara Desert

S and dunes stretching for miles
A s far as you can see
H ot and dry lands -
A ll the animals without the trees
R un from the scorching sun
A nd re-emerge when the dark sky comes with the midnight breeze.

Emily Holloway (9)
Grand Avenue Primary And Nursery School, Surbiton

Where My Books Take Me

Every time I pick up a book
I'm taken somewhere new
Whether it's war in 1940
Or somewhere I hear, "Mew!"
My books will always take me
Somewhere completely new.

Saaida Khan (9)
Grand Avenue Primary And Nursery School, Surbiton

The Emotions' Meanings

E nergetic

M adness

O rdinary

T iredness

I ntrigued

O ptimistic

N ervous

S adness.

Jackson Duggal (9)

Grand Avenue Primary And Nursery School, Surbiton

Halloween Has Come To An End

Halloween is here
Ready to spook you to death
Carving the pumpkins
Dress up so scary tonight
Because it may be the last.

Aiden Alagh (9)
Grand Avenue Primary And Nursery School, Surbiton

Animals

A lpaca

N ewt

I bis

M onkeys

A nteater

L emur

S ea monkeys.

Joe Parry (9)
Grand Avenue Primary And Nursery School, Surbiton

Bella

B eautiful
E nduring
L oving
L ovely
A dventurous.

Krisiya Angelova (9)

Grand Avenue Primary And Nursery School, Surbiton

Forgotten Paradise

As I walk across a lonely land,
Trees have fallen; it's dark and bland,
A masked masterpiece, a sheet disguised
By a forgotten and fragile paradise,
The sun does not shine on the crystal,
A dark and forgotten lake,
The trees don't grow on their spiky, splintered stakes.

Flowers do not blossom and the sun does not show,
The illuminated lake is mirrored by the crescent moon,
A resting delicacy
Does not know its place,
A forgotten paradise, far away.

A magical land,
A perfect picture with your toes in the sand,
Flowers cut one by one, perfectly, no mistakes,
But now it's gone, far away,
If only we could see such a forgotten paradise.

Archie Turner (11)
Hazlegrove School, Yeovil

What Lies Behind The Door?

She slowly approached the sacred tree,
Talisman in hand, clutching it with her life,
All thought lost in an endless sea,
A small bead of sweat trickled down her chin,
Her palms were so sweaty,
And her head was in a spin.
But she couldn't hold back, it was far too exciting,
She was still a little bit unsure,
And in her brain she was still deciding,
She chose to be brave and do it anyway,
Activating the talisman,
Something amazing came her way.

The roots of the tree wrapped around the trunk base,
Until they unfurled,
Where a door was placed,
But in a way, this door seemed special,
I don't know why.
Then it finally made sense, when the light started to
settle.
This door was left agape, some light shining through,
What would await her?
No one knew.

She took one more careful step,
Attempting to open the mysterious door,
Focused on a good mindset,
She held out a shaking hand,
And clasped her fingers around the handle,
It opened with a creaky sound.
Immediately, she was swept off her feet.
And went flying through the door,
It felt as though her heart skipped a beat.

After what seemed like ages,
She could feel solid ground beneath her feet.
But something had definitely changed,
Her surroundings had been modified,
Somehow, some way,
But she did not know why.
Her sight began to clear after a while,
Then her view was full with an amazing sight,
And on her face was a smile.

All she could see were magical things,
Each one full of wonder and majesty,
Was that a horse in the distance with wings?
The trees were made out of sparkling crystals,
The clouds were made of candyfloss,
And there was even a river of Skittles!

There were firebirds soaring overhead.

All so magical,
Her nerves stood on end,
All paths lined with chocolate mushrooms,
Flowers made of jelly,
And witches flying on brooms,
Bunnies popped out of holes,
Eating all the carrots.
Then under the bridge lived the trolls.
Many little huts all dotted around,
Everywhere you looked,
Elves walked about,
You could see burning fire over by the dragons,
Fairies flying everywhere.
Just look at the gnomes pulling the wagons.

She stood in awe at what she could see,
Rich in worth and value,
Definitely the best place to be,
This would be the perfect place, she thought,
To live my dreams and be myself.
Then, all her doubts and worries turned to naught,
She always wanted to adventure far,
To find new lands that amazed in wonder.
But how it came to her at the tree,

Behind a door that was revealed,
Something special for her to see.

What a great place to find yourself,
A magical land behind the door,
Ready to visit at a moment's notice,
An adventure to have you could be sure.

Hannah Manson (10)
Hazlegrove School, Yeovil

My Name Is Ted

My name is Ted
And I've banged my head
Which made me angry
And rather red.
Until it got better
And I was fine,
But I had a vendetta,
Against the vines!
I tripped on a vine
And smashed my head!
So, that was it for little old Ted!
So, I went back to the jungle,
Where I banged my head,
But this time,
I was happy,
'Cause I saw a rock wall I wanted to climb,
So, I ran over
And leapt on.
Before I knew it,
I slipped and got a great scare!

But do not worry,
Or sit and stare,
Because I was still there.

Just underneath the wall
Was a lake,
And I jumped in the lake
To have a break!
After my break,
I got back on,
But I was very scared,
Because my friends had gone!
So, I searched the jungle,
But I got lost
After, I found Fred,
And that was it for Fred and I, Ted!

Erin Reid (9)
Hazlegrove School, Yeovil

The Ancient Poem

I'm reading an ancient poem,
One never read before!
It's really very good,
So I want to read more.
As I flick through the pages,
I read every one.
Until I feel I'm not in my room,
And I'm completely gone!
I wake up in a different world,
I see a hummingbird.
It has a pencil in its beak
And writes a message,
Word by word.
It leads me to a dragon,
Deep inside a cave
And tells me a riddle,
Stage by stage by stage.
"What has a family,
And lots of love,
Like a twiggy nest,
Belonging to a dove?"

I think long and hard
Until, finally, I say: "Home!"
And I am back in bed!

Mathilda Bamsey (10)
Hazlegrove School, Yeovil

You Are...

You are the twinkle in the pond,
You are the sparkle in the river,
You are the spark in the stream,
You are good.

You are the glow in the rainbow,
You are the flash in my eye,
You are the glitter in the stars,
You are amazing.

You are the shine in the grass,
You are the glint in the sun,
You are the glitter in the moon,
You are you.

You are the shimmer in the trees,
You are the flicker in the flower,
You are the gleam in the leaf,
You are cool.

You are the dart of all,
You are the skip in the puddle,
You are the glide in the sky,
You are my heart.

Holly Tulk (11)
Hazlegrove School, Yeovil

A Winter's Morning

Snowflakes falling, twirling down
Spinning rapidly all around
A robin perching on a tree
Its chest as red as can be

A stark tree, standing all alone,
In the midst of winter, nothing's grown
The white-coated ground spreads for miles
As snow falls, pile upon pile

Frozen lakes glisten like stars
As animals hunt out in the dark
Icicles rattle in the breeze
As trees begin to lose their leaves

At morning, dusk, the air is so cold
Like winter will come - you won't be told
As flour stops making in the mill
Children are sledging down the hill.

Emilia Clark (11)
Hazlegrove School, Yeovil

Winter Day

W inter mornings, the frost glistens like sparkling diamonds

I nside the house, logs crackle furiously in the fireplace

N othing to be seen except the soft white snow

T rees are frozen with the cold like stone statues

E xtraordinary frozen lakes covered with children skating

R estless robins sing in the hedgerow

D ark, inky-black nights with sprinkling of glistening silver stars

A mazing mince pies, the delicious smell wafting up my nostrils

Y ou sip a mug of warm, thick hot chocolate, enjoying its warmth.

Cecilia Conaghan (10)
Hazlegrove School, Yeovil

The Tiger's Ways

Tiger, tiger, what a fright
He'll eat you up in the middle of the night
He'll prowl
He'll scowl
He'll give you a bite
But what do you do if you get in a fight?

They'll say to flee, to scurry, to dash
To scamper away from this scary cat
Be liked by him, or he'll take a swipe
Just remember these rules, and he should not bite

Now, that's how it goes
He'll keep you on your toes
Be careful out there
So, just take care
And always remember
Tiger, tiger, what a fright!

Alana Ward (10)
Hazlegrove School, Yeovil

Pets

Pets are really fun,
A great companion for everyone.
They are the light in the dark,
And they make great big farts.

Dogs are one of the best,
They easily beat the rest.
Always ready for a pat,
Much better than a cat.

Cats are cruel, nasty and mean,
At least they keep their fur clean.
Some of them are worse,
They will help a witch with a curse.

Big or small, creepy or cute,
Noisy or quiet, loud or mute.
The best friend I've ever met,
Everyone should have a pet.

Elysia Palmer (9)
Hazlegrove School, Yeovil

The Magic Lair

With a wish and a swish,
A dragon appeared,
That blew mouthfuls of fire,
It roared and raged,
But never tired.

Everlasting bubble streams,
Floated through the cavern lair,
With rare animals jumping with a playful air,
A graceful phoenix swooped through the magic lair,
With wings as bright as a ruby-red flare.

Unicorns grazed peacefully,
Under a dazzling diamond tree,
While fairies skimmed the waterfall,
And dived down into the crystal-clear pool.

Clementine Cerri (10)
Hazlegrove School, Yeovil

The Last Midnight Dragon

Glowing over the midnight sea,
Stands the most beautiful of dragons.

Its wings merge into the night sky like they're see-
through, and its tail waves around rapidly,
Shimmering beneath the stars.

He lives beneath the depths of the water,
Where no sunlight can be seen,
Eating salty, slimy fish left behind from its prey.

Its eyes glimmer among the dark sky,
Like shooting stars in the depths of night.
And his teeth are very small, shiny and very sharp!

Elsa Sempele (8)
Hazlegrove School, Yeovil

Rhinoceros

R hinos run on their toes
H ere in the desert, rhinos munch on leaves
I n the Savannah, rhinos are alive
N ever will a rhino go near the scent of man
O n their heads is a horn so strong
C rash is a group of rhinos living together
E ars twitch when they sense danger
R eady to charge at its prey
O ff to muddy pools to cool
S tomping their feet to play.

Neve Corthorn (9)
Hazlegrove School, Yeovil

Hockey

H ockey - a sport with a ball and a stick, where kids show off their tricks

O ver the goal the parents scream, to dream, to win and then they sing!

C ool ball skills which kids thrill to tally and end up to rally

K ids smack balls at top bins and the goalkeeper does a spin

E qual scores are just a bore

Y es, get in! You score, then you draw and everyone's bored!

Barnaby Edgar (11)
Hazlegrove School, Yeovil

Puppies!

P uppies are so cute, everyone will agree.

U nder the Christmas tree in winter they play.

P erfect pets for everyone, you would say.

P eople will go to the shops to buy one.

I n the park, you can play and have fun.

E xciting, playful, graceful, funny and more.

S ome people only know what's in store.

Martha Cape (9)

Hazlegrove School, Yeovil

Animals

A ntelopes bound on the plains of Africa
N ewts glide in the streams of Eastern India
I guanas lie in the treetops of Mexico
M acaws soar on the edges of the Caribbean
A lligators slide in the depths of the USA
L eopards leap in the mountains of North-East Africa
S now foxes pounce around in Canada.

Iris Richards (9)
Hazlegrove School, Yeovil

Seasons

S easons are different times in the year

E very season is different

A leaf falls down from a tree and makes a crunching sound

S now falls in winter and sleet squelches

O n spring days, it becomes a bit brighter

N ot least, but last is...

S ummer is the season to enjoy playing outside in the sun.

Clemmie Lindsay-Clark (9)

Hazlegrove School, Yeovil

A Balancing Act

School is like a balancing act,
It can be good and it can be bad.
For example, drama is the best of all,
Whilst rugby is definitely not my call.

Swimming is like a balancing act,
It can be good and it can be bad.
For example, sometimes we get free swims,
But other times, we just get sore limbs.

Henry (Harry) Gould (11)
Hazlegrove School, Yeovil

The Fiery Fox

The fiery fox leaps on my lap
It runs around chasing bats
Making trails
And flapping tails
Is all it loves to do.

The fiery fox loves eating rodents
It beat all its opponents
Skipping through the autumn leaves
Chewing up jumpers with sleeves
Is all it loves to do.

Zara Cookson (11)
Hazlegrove School, Yeovil

My Dream

Once I dreamt
That I spent
All my money
On a bunny.
The bunny was remarkably light,
It decided to flee,
So I giggled with glee.
Now I'm stuck in a big tragedy
Because the bunny ate the kite
And the kite ate the bunny, you see,
It's really not funny.

Ella Chiswell (10)
Hazlegrove School, Yeovil

Football

Ninety minutes of rough and tough
To see who wins, you may have a huff.

Playing in the streets or on a pitch
If you're good, you might end up rich.

You could get hurt
Or covered in dirt.

Put on your shin pads and boots
And dig in to your roots.

Blake Williams (11)
Hazlegrove School, Yeovil

Autumn

A ll the leaves fall from the trees
U sually, children play and cannon leaves like confetti
T rick or treat?
U nder trees are chilling conkers
M any mammals hibernate in soft shelters
N ormally ghosts say, "Boo!" Did I scare you?

Grace Britten (9)

Hazlegrove School, Yeovil

Bonfire Night

The heat hits me like an oven
The flames are dancing devils
The fire goes *bang, crackle, sizzle*
And the sparks reach out at me.

The atmosphere is like a party
The darkness makes everyone cheer
And I want it to never end.

Harry Entwistle (11)
Hazlegrove School, Yeovil

Special Space

S pecial space, with all the non-explored,
P lace of wonder, where UFOs have soared,
A rchitecture of planets, all shapes and sizes,
C reation of magnificence that could win prizes,
E xplored - not - of this amazing place.

Clementine Whitfield (9)

Hazlegrove School, Yeovil

Flower

F lowers are full of fun
L ittle lilies lying on lily pads
O pening buds hot with colour
W ind whispering around wisteria
E vergreen trees forever growing
R ed raspberries for eating.

Eve Binmore (10)

Hazlegrove School, Yeovil

Sleepless Nights

Sleepless nights,
And endless fights,
For equal rights,
At many local sights.

Like Rosa Parks,
Who made remarks,
Or Martin Luther King,
Who stood for everything.

Oliver Dando (11)
Hazlegrove School, Yeovil

The Earth Is Round From Outer Space

We see trees are green,
And in-between,
A light blue sea without a sound,
Stars and galaxies,
Moons and planets,
From what's known as the Milky Way.

Harrietta Brooks (9)
Hazlegrove School, Yeovil

Krieg Der Welt (War Of The World)

Constant anxiety fills my faithless mind
As I worry about my affectionate family.
Being homesick takes over me.
I carefully trudge through the mass of sludge
Making sure not to slip.
Minutes,
The power of endless hours,
I want to go home.

A large, yellow wall comes towards my trench.
Should I run?
Would I run?
I duck down in my trench and can feel the weight of
thousands of heavy particles.
I cover my dry mouth with my ripped, filthy uniform.
"I can't see! My eyes. I can't see!" screams a man in
distress a few metres away from me.
Minutes,
The power of endless hours,
I want to go home.

Whizz! Bang! Thud!
The obsidian-black bombs screech as they make the
world tremble.

They are furious creatures seeking revenge.
We charge through the narrow miles-long trench.
Mud is grabbing at my feet like desperate hands.
Minutes,
The power of endless hours,
I want to go home.

Rattling rifles rapidly firing.
Sandbags as heavy as boulders.
Everything seems so important now.
Minutes,
The power of endless hours,
I want to go home.

Emma Short (10)
John Emmerson Batty Primary School, Redcar

I Don't Get Paid Enough For This!

March after march,
Demand after demand,
Hell after hell,
Echoes of horror scatter into the air,
When will this hell-like prison end?

Dots of running figures,
Dash away from this yellow-like wall,
Spreading larger and larger on,
When will this hell-like prison end?

Crack and thump,
Of fiery bullets,
Roaring at you,
Ducking down,
Not up,
Of the fear of the bombs,
So don't be scared,
It's war,
When will this hell-like prison end?

The mud is a land grabbing at our feet,
Squelch, squish, squelch, squish,

Day after day,
Night after night,
Hours drag as an infinite life,
When will this hell-like prison end?

The whistle,
Of the time,
Where we all dance for our lives
The thunderous bang,
We don't have time to look around,
Crash, smash,

When will this hell-like prison end?

Anessa Hutchinson (10)
John Emmerson Batty Primary School, Redcar

Where The War Began!

Violently, the bombs were shaking the ground,
As the soldiers were marching through,
Bang! Pop! Thud!
Anxiously marching through the wet mud,
Watching their friends die, almost sobbing,
But they were able to hold it back,
Every minute thinking, *when will this end or will it end?*

A long time ago, in a world with no fight,
Brave soldiers marched on with their might,
In muddy trenches, they lived day by day and
They stood between the walls of mud,
They wrote home with their love.

Bang!
In the muddy, old trenches where soldiers would stay,
A yellow substance of smoke came in,
The soldiers dragged their heads down,
But in the distance, they could hear,
"Help! I can't see. He-"
Bang!

The squelching mud grabbed their feet,
Wondering, *when will the war end or will it end?*

The nights were cold and the days were long,
But they kept it together and stayed strong.

Millie Richards (10)
John Emmerson Batty Primary School, Redcar

The Fallen Soldier

The sound of gunshots
Filled the air,
Ears ringing, heart pounding,
But even louder was the sound of the whistle,
Putting a halt to the endless racket.
I was glad to escape the waterfalls of mud in the trench.
Soldiers fumbled up the ladder like ferrets
And rifles were grasped tight.
I pulled myself up and crawled behind a rock.

Just then, a man bellowed in pain,
"I'm bleeding! I'm bleeding! Help me!"
I dragged him toward me and covered the wound.
The eyes of my friend went pale.
He lay there, lifeless.

Whizz! Bang!
Bombs exploded in giant clouds of dust.
I dragged his corpse into the trench.
Me and another man dredged him
And left his body in the trench.
There was no time to say goodbye.

Jerry Overfield (11)
John Emmerson Batty Primary School, Redcar

Trauma Of The War

Stuck in monstrous mud,
Nervously, we trudge,
Our feet being grabbed by sludge,
Standing for days on end,
Will I ever escape this hell?

Monsters roam life-threatening lands,
Bullets screaming,
Bombs roaring,
Watching... stalking... hiding...
Gas creeps towards us
Will I ever escape this hell?

Every second counts,
God... Please save us,
Fire screeching at my feet,
No more food to eat,
Uncontrollable shaking,
Will I ever escape this hell?

Losing track of days,
Losing track of time,
Losing myself to the pain,
I won't ever escape,
This traumatic hell...

Ava Riddiough (11)
John Emmerson Batty Primary School, Redcar

Horrors Of War

Waist-deep in sludge, we eternally hobble.
Whizz! Pop! Bang!
"Run, boys, run!"
Screams of horror echo through the land.
The wall has returned!
Choking, suffocating, gasping for air.
What will happen next, fate will decide.

People shaking uncontrollably
Corpses lying down. Mud grabbing their feet.
The smell of death fills the air.
What will happen next, fate will decide.

Buckets and buckets of water piling up
Rotten food all mushy and green
The starving men, barely alive
Rats as big as cats roaming the trenches
What will happen next, fate will decide.

Josh Scrafton (11)
John Emmerson Batty Primary School, Redcar

Realities Of War

Rescuing friends
When will this end?
Stomping through sludge,
Thud, thump, thud,
Emerge, boys, quick!

When will we sleep?
When will we eat?
When will we be free from this prodigious pain?

The yellow wall,
Marched towards us,
The unprepared men's shrieks,
Soared over us,
Emerge, boys, quick!

Mud clawed at our feet,
Bugs scratched at our bodies,
When will we be free from this prodigious pain?

Bloodshot eyes,
We fought on through it,
Boom, crash, fire...

Olivia Griffiths (10)
John Emmerson Batty Primary School, Redcar

When Will I Get Home?

Gunshots fill the sky, *pop! Bang! Crash!*
Soldiers beg for mercy
Nightmares absorb me
Bullets are like the devil's friend
Ears popping, pounding headaches

A large yellow wall marches towards us
Soldiers scream and panic
Thousands of dead soldiers lie in front of me
When will this treacherous nightmare end?

Family start to panic and worry
Everyone hates it here
I miss my family
Soldiers lie in pain
Is my family fine?
When will I get home?

Keaton Sarginson (11)
John Emmerson Batty Primary School, Redcar

Danger Is Happening!

Lying in pain
Crying or help
Sludge grabbing at my feet like angry hands
I miss home

Bombs screaming
Bullets squeaking
Men lying dead
I miss home

Homesick
Sending letters forwards and backwards
Visions of dead bodies
I miss home

Yellow clouds seize me
Gasping for breath
Nervously, I run
I miss home

Trenches flooded
Soldiers wet and cold
Boom, pop, whizz
I miss home.

Paige Keen (11)
John Emmerson Batty Primary School, Redcar

An Owl

A haiku

Eerie jump-scaring.
Some loud, resounding screeching.
An owl that's screaming.

Olive Wileman (9)

John Emmerson Batty Primary School, Redcar

Hogwarts

A haiku

Firm upon a mound
With the danger, lost and found
I am Hogwarts' grounds.

Zachary Hubbard (9)

John Emmerson Batty Primary School, Redcar

Quidditch

A haiku

Three unique, rough balls,
House Cup causes many falls,
Game in Wizard Laws.

Sophie Dowey (9)
John Emmerson Batty Primary School, Redcar

Sorting Hat

A haiku

Grand and special hat
Dull, sharp and tight inside it
Great hat on a mat.

Jaxon Cook (10)
John Emmerson Batty Primary School, Redcar

A Potion

A haiku

Lethal and dingy
Blood first tastes abnormal deaths
The potion of death.

Jackson West (9)

John Emmerson Batty Primary School, Redcar

Quidditch

A haiku

Balls are not the same
It finds wizards lots of fame
The beautiful game!

Harvey Robinson (9)
John Emmerson Batty Primary School, Redcar

A Wizard

A haiku

Wearing wonky hats
Beards like the tails of rats
Wizards that are cats.

Elenore Cooke (9)

John Emmerson Batty Primary School, Redcar

Owls

A haiku

Magical white owl
Colossal, wide, maroon eyes
Lightning-fast wise owl.

Matthew Compton (9)

John Emmerson Batty Primary School, Redcar

A Cat

A haiku

Fleecy, silky hair,
Will attack without a care,
A calm cat is rare.

Finley Jones (10)
John Emmerson Batty Primary School, Redcar

A Potion

A haiku

Ensnaring the mind
Its silvery elixir
With cloudy mixture.

Esme Evans (9)

John Emmerson Batty Primary School, Redcar

The Magic Of Happiness

There is one big spark inside,
Think about the colours that don't want to hide.
The colours that you picked seem alright,
The colours that seem to be very light.

Let me see a gorgeous smile,
That I've definitely not seen for a while,
I really want to know how you feel,
So let us all go for a family meal!

Now I can see you gaze,
Although it was a bit of a challenging maze,
But now that you feel happy and fun,
We could all go and have a cinnamon bun!

Amber Perkins (8)
Larkfield Primary School, Southport

My Real Hero

He is my real hero,
Who helps me in my study.
Who gives me some time to play.

He is my hero,
Who loves me so much.
He is my real hero,
He is my dad.

He makes me happy,
When I am so sad.
He makes me confident,
When I am so nervous.

He is my real hero,
He is my dad.

He is the best in my life,
He is my real hero.
He is my dad.

Redwana Shamsia (10)
Larkfield Primary School, Southport

Friends

Friends are there to look out for you,
They make you smile, even if they haven't visited for a while,
Friends are kind and you can make plans together,
They will be with you forever and ever,

Friends are like the colours of the rainbow,
Their friendship makes you feel sunny and bright,
With them by your side, you will feel alright,
And may you be a good friend to others.

Eleanor Wright (9)
Larkfield Primary School, Southport

My Extraordinary Hamster

My hamster looks like a tiny little panther
With her small paws and her cute claws
She climbs so high, I think one day
She might be able to touch the sky!
My hamster is so fast she's like the Flash!
She eats cheese and carrots
She's almost like a rabbit.
She runs all day in her wheel
But sleeps all night by my side.

Kai Goldring-Jones (9)
Larkfield Primary School, Southport

Autumnal Sky

The sky is dark and the air is cold,
Red and orange leaves fall down to the floor,
People are wrapped up nice and warm,
Dogs wear fleeces to keep them dry,
Cats curl up by the glowing warm fires,
Smells surround - of bonfires and fireworks,
Rain may fall but smiles are warm,
Sipping hot cocoa, we enjoy the autumnal sky.

Caleigh Jones (9)
Larkfield Primary School, Southport

Fred Is Under My Bed!

There is a monster under my bed.
And I believe his name is Fred.
With wretched teeth and golden eyes.
I think he's after my French fries!

He sometimes yells and gives a screech.
However, I have never heard him speak.
He stays under my bed until I'm asleep.
But I'm not scared as he is really sweet.

Oliver Haughton (10)
Larkfield Primary School, Southport

My Cats

M y cats run up and down around the house
Y ou won't survive without an attack at night

C ats have so much energy when they're little
A t night is their mad hour, running, fighting
T onight they'll strike again!
S urprising me with purrs early in the morning.

Matthew Stark (10)
Larkfield Primary School, Southport

The Life Of Kittens

K icking my brothers and sisters when we are playing
I think it's sleepy time, zzz
T ickles, I love them on my tummy
T ime for food, mmm
E xtra noisy, especially at nighttime
N ighttime or is it actually playtime?
S ocks as white as snow.

Arabella Woods (7)
Larkfield Primary School, Southport

Space

In space, there are planets and galaxies galore,
The Milky Way is full of glimmering colours I adore.
As rockets fly by Earth as fast as lightning,
I think, *can I be an astronaut and fly to the space station?*
In space the stars are on fire,
But on Earth they are spectacular dots in the night sky.

Noah Taylor (9)
Larkfield Primary School, Southport

Winter

Winter, Christmastime
Everyone excited
Exciting feeling in the air
It starts to snow
People building snowmen
Making snow angels
People celebrating with family and friends
December till February
School's back
It starts to get wet
That's winter!

Ryan Ogden (10)
Larkfield Primary School, Southport

Dext

D exter is my doggy
E ating my sister's socks
X ander is his best friend
T hey love to play together.

Sometimes he barks at night
And scratches at my door
But I don't mind that much
Because I love him to the moon and back.

Ethan Webster (10)
Larkfield Primary School, Southport

The Speedy Hamster

My hamster is fast
He always wants to be in his yellow ball
He always makes me smile
He's my lovely hamster

His name is Speedo
He always escapes
He nibbles my fingers and toes
He eats fast and runs fast
He's my best friend!

Declan Ejchart (10)
Larkfield Primary School, Southport

Summer Air

Summer air is nice and sweet,
On the pier, I can smell the salty sea,
Children run, having fun,
People like walking their dogs,
And families getting fish and chips,
Colourful kites soar high on the beach,
Summer air is nice and sweet.

Connie Dempster (9)
Larkfield Primary School, Southport

Pets

Stripe is a guinea pig.
He is small and fluffy.
At night, he is cosy.
In the summer, he is happy.
In the winter, he is sad.

Like a meatball, he is nice.
Sometimes he nibbles my fingers.
When he is grumpy, he bites me.

Melissa Wright (9)
Larkfield Primary School, Southport

The Four Seasons

T he perfect hot cross bun from Greggs
H oping for lots of Easter eggs
E arly spring, new birth

F resh flower buds that grow from the earth
O verwhelmingly hot
U nfortunately, the ice cream melts in a pot
R idiculously high, the sun flies in the sky

S unbathing happily, at the beach you lie
E ventually, harvest comes with a cold breeze
A utumn leaves dropping from deciduous trees
S weets and freaks, trick-or-treat
O bnoxious-looking pumpkins that will make your heart beat
N on-stop snow appears in the air
S anta Claus delivers presents everywhere.

Elsie Brundell (9)
Mendlesham Primary School, Mendlesham

Emotion Explosion

Excited is good to be,
Memories make you feel free.
Overwhelmed is rather unpleasant,
Terrified is not at all pleasant.

Ignorance is especially mean,
Overjoyed feels like a dream.
Nervousness feels weird to me,
Emotions everyone needs to be.

X-rays give you quite a fright,
Personal diaries feel right.
Love makes you feel warm,
Overexcitement happens at dawn.

Troubled feelings can't be good,
Intrigued by a magazine or book.
Outraged by a person who is rude,
Nonchalant and feeling like a dude.

Isla Clements (10)
Mendlesham Primary School, Mendlesham

The School Run

He would arrive with an arm for a hug
And a bag full of sweets.
I'd say, "Please can I have a sweet before school?
We don't have to tell Dad we're breaking the rules."
He would bring the jams that I loved most,
So I could sample them on four rounds of toast.
Sometimes he'd say,
"Can I come to school with you?
It's Fishy Friday and fish and chips are on the menu."
Taking me to school is the thing I most miss,
I wish I could have just one more kiss.

Edith Cornell (9)
Mendlesham Primary School, Mendlesham

Our Habitat

N ever drop litter in a wood,

A lways litter pick, that is good!

T ell them not to cut down trees,

U nderstand we need them to breathe.

R emember to look among the trees, see our land and love the breeze.

E njoy our wood and love the pond, appreciate where we all belong.

Lucia Faliveno (8)
Mendlesham Primary School, Mendlesham

Our Beautiful World

Over the lands and in the seas,
Lots of animals you shall see.

Bunnies to whales, ears to tails.

Slithering, skipping and hopping,
Swimming, flying and trotting.

Bringing joy to our beautiful world.

Harrison Clements (10)
Mendlesham Primary School, Mendlesham

The White Winter Fox

The white winter fox moves swiftly through the night,
As the white winter fox comes with a fright.
When it goes silent with no trace,
The little white fox sees an unfamiliar face.
The little white fox prances through the air,
As the white winter fox runs everywhere.

The white winter fox gets utterly tired,
As the white winter fox comes across a fence of wires.
The poor tired fox jumps curiously over the wired fence,
As it sees three trees which is pretty intense.
They are tall and grand and so very old,
As the little white fox hears a voice saying, "Behold!"

The white winter fox finds a perfect tree,
As it goes inside to see if it will be happy.
Thump goes the little fox's paw,
That carefully touches the ground of the tree floor.
It curls up in a ball,
As it looks up at the wonderful tree wall.
When it hears no sound of anybody.

As the little winter fox goes to sleep,
Its tail goes around its body,
It doesn't make a peep and has a wonderful sleep.

Sophia Bywater (9)
Meole Brace Church Of England Primary And Nursery, Shrewsbury

Super, Amazing Space

Space is a freezing dark place full of gigantic galaxies.
Bright shining stars hotter than boiling water.
The sun, the hottest thing around,
Floating miles away from planet Earth,
Surrounded by a force field-like atmosphere,
Keeping the planet warm.

Our beautiful solar system has eight different planets.
Mercury, Venus, Earth, Mars,
Jupiter, Saturn, Uranus and Neptune.
All different sizes!
Mercury is closest to the sun.
Boiling hot day and night,
And it's dark grey.
Venus is second in line,
Even hotter than the rest of the planets.
It's covered in volcanos that erupt all the time.
Neptune is the last planet in line.
It's the coldest, the windiest and made out of ice!

There are two circles of asteroids in the solar system.
The Asteroid Belt and the Kuiper Belt.
Both completely grey.
They're full of asteroids,

So the belts of asteroids,
Are too dangerous to go through.

Elliot Taylor (9)
Meole Brace Church Of England Primary And Nursery, Shrewsbury

The Sad, Sad Poem

The luscious trees are being damaged,
Animals' survival shelters being destroyed,
Hedges burning and screaming, tears of pain,
Plants wilting slower and slower and slower,
Monkeys screeching as loud as sirens of despair,
Parents of babies are disorientated,
Animals screeching, like spider monkeys,
Trees falling as fast as rockets shooting in space,
The poor homeless animals are now unsafe,

Fire as huge as skyscrapers,
Bugs and beetles as petite as atoms,
Ash cloud as thick as glue,
The ash-filled sky is no longer blue,
Canopy trees collapsing,
The deer and herbivores no longer have food,
The colourful bright toucans dying,
The dark soil has been poisoned,
Emergent trees being cut down,
The ground is turning grey.

Ayomide Dawodu (9)
Meole Brace Church Of England Primary And Nursery, Shrewsbury

Magical Space Constellations Riddle

It's as bright as the sun and the moon.
It's as big as ten stars and it glimmers.
As colourful as a patchwork blanket.
It's as wide as two trees together.
It's as pretty as rubies and lapis lazuli.
Constellations fly past it like rockets.
It's almost impossible to see because it blends in.
It's as rare as emeralds and diamonds.

It blends in with the stars and light.
It's as exclusive as a luxury boat.
It's as beautiful as the galaxy.
It shines at night but not at day.

It shines like the sun and gives you luck like never before.
It looks like a good luck charm because it is ultra rare.

It's the glory of a supernova!

Oliver Roughan (8)
Meole Brace Church Of England Primary And Nursery, Shrewsbury

My Incredible Exploding Friend

My exploding friend explodes when they are worried
about something,
One time, we stepped in a puddle,
Which got us in a muddle,
Because it splashed in our eyes,
So we couldn't see,
So we ran into the sea,
Me and my incredible exploding friend!
I sang and sang,
And they rang and rang the bell on top of the tower,
But then they fell, still ringing the bell,
So I caught them and they exploded and I went with
them,
And somehow we became Romans
Then I realised my friend can explode and time travel,
So we kept singing and ringing,
Until we exploded again,
We went into the future with flying cars,

Me and my incredible exploding friend!

Bess Dargan (8)
Meole Brace Church Of England Primary And Nursery, Shrewsbury

Geography

G eography is a subject that people learn at school,

E cuador is a country in South America close to the vast, blue ocean,

O man is in Asia next to Saudi Arabia and the UAE,

G abon is as big as Guinea and it is in Africa,

R omania is not bigger than the UK but can attract lots of people,

A fghanistan has a capital named Kabul and it's a large country,

P hilippines is the twelfth most populated country and it is an island nation,

H aiti is an island next to the country of the Dominican Republic,

Y emen is the only country that starts with the letter 'Y'.

Marcus Macam (8)
Meole Brace Church Of England Primary And Nursery, Shrewsbury

Harry Potter World

H arry Potter World was the best day for me,
A mazing, exciting, extraordinary,
R eady for the day,
R eady, on the way,
Y es! Let's clap and shout hooray!

P etite amounts of fog,
O ver where the Death Eaters are,
T urn around and you will see Ron's flying car!
T ime went quickly for me,
E veryone looked so happy,
R eally fun!

W ow! It was exciting,
O ver there I could see Harry Potter,
R on and his brother,
L aughing with his mother,
D estiny to stay with each other!

Imogen Lancaster (8)
Meole Brace Church Of England Primary And Nursery, Shrewsbury

Christmas Delights

Putting on my slippers to go open my presents
Mum and Dad are in the living room there for me
Mum cooking the turkey, Dad making the stuffing
Me waiting to greet the guests into our nice home
Me in my pyjamas getting nice and cosy
Looking at the Christmas tree standing like a soldier
Mum shouts, "Dinner's ready!" and everyone races to
the table

Finishing my Christmas dinner
Playing fun board games
Me and my brother falling out
But then laughing together
Mum and Dad sipping a big bottle of champagne
Me and my brother forgive each other
And then drift off.

Kamica Edmunds (9)
Meole Brace Church Of England Primary And Nursery, Shrewsbury

The Colourful Candyland

Do you like sweets and treats?
Then go to Candyland, as sweet as can be
You can see all the rainbow in just one look
Trees, bees, all edible and it's incredible
You have left the world behind you, stay all night
Just don't get eaten by the mighty frighty crew.

You can sleep in a bed of chocolate
Everyone agrees it is the perfect place to be
Spinning because they're winning
Eating sweets and treats
All day, all night, just don't get a fright.

There is just one twist
Don't get carried away
Otherwise the creepy clowns will bite...

Lydia Talbot (8)
Meole Brace Church Of England Primary And Nursery, Shrewsbury

The Football Poem

Football is awesome and exciting,
It's as noisy as a jet,
The players run as fast as a cheetah,
Always trying to score!
The football moves across the pitch,
It's round like the moon,
Football is challenging,
It's hard to learn the tricks and skills,
The ball dribbles like a baby,
You get better at free kicks,
And penalties,
Heading the ball is as hard as a brick!
When the ball goes to your head, it hurts,
The goalies are there to save the ball,
They dive like a dolphin,
In a match, two teams meet,
They pass to their teammates.

Mason Pritchard-Evans (8)
Meole Brace Church Of England Primary And Nursery, Shrewsbury

Being With My Friends

Running speedily away from the tagger
Then we have fun
Playing with the equipment and with hoops
Using skipping ropes and balls
Jumping over a skipping rope
You catch the ball with your hands
We got more stuff like scoops and rockets
Playing with the equipment
Playing with my friends
Playing more, running and tag
Different games like Chicken or Hero

Happy and laughing with my friends
Nobody sad, and nobody left out
Just playing with each other
Running and running
Happier and happier
Nobody left out!

Jack Shaw-Rawlings (9)
Meole Brace Church Of England Primary And Nursery, Shrewsbury

The Super Sea Story!

The blue sparkling sea shines in the sun,
While people are having fun.
Underneath the sun,
There's trouble going on.

Fish are swimming fast,
While sharks are coming past.
Dolphins are having fun,
Like people in the sun.
The sea is very clear,
But no one knows sharks are near.

The sea is calm,
People are doing it harm.
Glowing fish,
You'll never miss.

All the animals are happy,
As the baby dolphins have a nappy.
The turtles feel sad,
And all the other animals feel bad.

Sophie Edgerton (8)
Meole Brace Church Of England Primary And Nursery, Shrewsbury

The Big Climb!

As I was walking through the woods
I found an old climbing frame that was as tall as a tree
I wanted to climb it but there were no steps.
Then, I found a wooden door.
I smashed it open
The steps were on the inside.
I noticed a scroll that said 'funtastic, fabulous gold'.

As I went onto a step,
It turned into a solid gold bar.
I continued my climb but was left feeling disappointed
Not all of them turned into solid gold.
Fifteen minutes later at the top
There was no gold but I didn't know I had the lot.

Jesse Lee (8)
Meole Brace Church Of England Primary And Nursery, Shrewsbury

Magical Riddles

I'm as huge as an elephant
And I'm quite elegant.
I breathe hot fire
And the colour is glistening ember.
What am I?

Answer: A dragon.

I can sing like a lovely bird
And by the way, I can be heard.
I've got a shiny fish tail
And look at my lovely scales.
What am I?

Answer: A mermaid.

I can turn you into stone
And I like to hear you groan.
My favourite animal is a snake
And they don't like cake.
What am I?

Answer: A gorgon.

Louie McDowall (9)
Meole Brace Church Of England Primary And Nursery, Shrewsbury

The Grizzly Bear's Story

G ently strolling through the winter breeze,
R ed holly appearing, dancing through the night,
I ntense, incredible white snow,
Z igzagging carefully to follow the bright glow,
Z ooming through the dark, quiet night,
L onging to get a long-living life,
Y elling in the wide open space.

B uried all warm in a dark, gloomy cave,
E ntering a long, deep sleep, now all peaceful,
A ll is well for now,
R esting till the winter's been put to bed.

Amira Gregory (8)
Meole Brace Church Of England Primary And Nursery, Shrewsbury

The Night Before Christmas

The sky is full of stars.
Snowflakes are falling.
The children are waiting for their presents.
The moon is shining so bright while Santa is busy flying.
The elves are delivering presents quickly.
Santa is eating quietly.
Bells are making a lot of noise.
Lots of the toys are plastic toys.
Tick-tock! Tick-tock! Tick-tock!
The children are half awake, waiting for Santa to arrive.
The reindeer are getting tired fast.
Santa is singing Christmas songs to keep the reindeer moving.

Sienna Evans (9)

Meole Brace Church Of England Primary And Nursery, Shrewsbury

Spooky Halloween

Spiders crawl through their webs.
Poisonous potions glimmer through the night.
Owls hoot through the night.
Ooh, ghosts are awake.
Crypt of the dead.
Yelling out in my head.

Haunted houses have a lot of graves.
And my candy starts to come alive.
Lonely skeletons in the dark.
Looking scary in the park.
Oh as I take my candy out of the bowl.
Werewolves run out.
Evil demons run past.
Eek, I jump and gasp,
Now I hate Halloween, I'm so glad it's lapsed.

Evie Walker (8)
Meole Brace Church Of England Primary And Nursery, Shrewsbury

Bad Dreams

My friends wake up.
I know that in your dreams, you see the way the world
should be,
But we breathe in reality.
Your dreams won't stay peaceful,
Even through a whisper of evil,
And there is evil in the minds of sleeping people.
Wake up!
There you go!
Wipe the sleep from your eyes,
A rise in replies for those cries.
Tell them we despise lies
From a hateful enterprise.
Tell them that dream where nobody dies
And no one gets hurt.

Darcy Hustwayte (8)
Meole Brace Church Of England Primary And Nursery, Shrewsbury

Hedgehog Hibernation

Coming, running, as fast as a cheetah.
The tall, lush grass swayed like a storm.
As a tiny, swift hedgehog ran through it,
Swift as a bird,
Swift as a cheetah,
Swift as a snake.
Bang! Bang! Bang!
Over the hills the ancient tree rose.
Then... *bang!*
As slow as a slug, leaves fell from the sky.
As the hedgehog looked up, the tree waved.
As comfortable as a dog.
Like a pitch-black cave.
All around, orange, teeny leaves fell.
Safe!
For now,
Goodnight!

Benjamin Harrison (8)
Meole Brace Church Of England Primary And Nursery, Shrewsbury

The Maestro From Brussels

King Kevin is the master at free kicks.
He plays for City, a Premier League team that wins lots
and lots of trophies. This player is so energetic, swift
and talented.
He plays for Belgium and scores lots of goals for his
country.
His country plays in the World Cup and Euros for City.
He is the captain and lifts all of the trophies.
I insist he is wonderful,
I insist he is absolutely brilliant.
Kevin De Bruyne is truly the best.

Finley Greer (9)
Meole Brace Church Of England Primary And Nursery, Shrewsbury

The Greatest Of All Time

O llie Watkins scored a bicycle kick.
L eaps up and scored a header.
L eaps up and saves it.
I like to be midfield.
E nergetic and a shield.

W ater for the match.
A ggressive, I won't latch.
T ackling the opponent.
K ick back and attack.
I t was a good match.
N ext match is soon.
S kills to improve, I'm over the moon.

Jack Sanders (9)
Meole Brace Church Of England Primary And Nursery, Shrewsbury

The Day I Went To The Zoo

The day I went to the zoo,
I saw an elephant do a poo.
He saw me through the glass,
And charged through the grass.
Then I saw a monkey,
That looked very chunky.
There was an ape,
That was eating a grape.
After that, I saw a bat,
That was eating a rat on the mat,
In the middle of the farm that belonged to Pat.
After talking to Pat,
I saw a mat that had a fat cat,
Sitting right on top.

Roman Oliver (8)
Meole Brace Church Of England Primary And Nursery, Shrewsbury

The White Wolf

T eeny, tiny paws.
H uge, shimmering eyes.
E legant, joyful spirit.

W onderful, peaceful morning.
H eated, fresh sun.
I ntelligent, beautiful sky.
T all, swaying grass.
E vergreen, gigantic trees.

W ise, adorable wolf pup.
O bservant, quiet young cub.
L ittle, lonely baby wolf.
F riendly, graceful fluff ball.

Merryn Baker (8)
Meole Brace Church Of England Primary And Nursery, Shrewsbury

Adorable Animals

Cute rabbits going *crunch, crunch, crunch,*
Huge dogs going *munch, munch, munch,*
Tiny hamsters crawling,
Gigantic humans bawling,

Cheetahs running fast,
Whilst cats are crawling past,
The puppies are oh-so fluffy,
But rabbits are not so puffy,

The hamsters are so calm,
But the dog is lost on the farm,
The guinea pigs are sad,
When the other animals feel bad.

Ayda Dawson (8)
Meole Brace Church Of England Primary And Nursery, Shrewsbury

A Trip To Wembley

There once was a boy called Owen,
He was on his way to Wembley,
In the car, the phone rang,
Liverpool wanted him to play.

Quickly he said yes,
He got treated to VIP,
He put the goalkeeper top on,
And ran out to the pitch.

At half-time, he was losing,
In the second half, he made a comeback,
He made an outstanding save,
Then he scored two more times.

Owen Mellor (9)
Meole Brace Church Of England Primary And Nursery, Shrewsbury

Golden Baller Messi

Hello, I am Messi,
I am one of the best footballers in the world.
I am healthy, brave and rapid.
I like playing football more than anything,
I get the ball and score!
I am playing now.
Pass, pass the ball!
Yes, goal!
One-nil!
Martinez with a great save
Kept this alive.
Goal from Messi, that was a golden goal!
Golden baller, winner of lots of trophies.

Juke Williams (9)
Meole Brace Church Of England Primary And Nursery, Shrewsbury

Boom! Boom! Benson Boone

His music is loved by millions
Boom! Boom! Benson Boone

His music makes me feel happy
Dance! Dance! Benson Boone

The beat is beautiful
Dance! Dance! Benson Boone

Turn up the volume
Sing! Sing! Benson Boone

Singers like Boone like to make you dance
Benson Boone runs like an angry tiger across the stage
Sing! Sing! Benson Boone.

Lacey Seyffert (8)
Meole Brace Church Of England Primary And Nursery, Shrewsbury

Theme Parks Fun

T all, fast rides,
H appy memories,
E xciting roller coasters,
M arvellous sights,
E nthusiastic people.

P eople eating sweets,
A rray of games,
R apid rides,
K eeping calm,
S lightly dizzy.

F antastic prizes,
U nbeatable fun,
N ever wanting to leave.

Romy Hales (9)
Meole Brace Church Of England Primary And Nursery, Shrewsbury

Magical Majestic Water Dragon

Scary and unknown
Is the deep,
People say it's a
Dragon's home,
Because whenever
Fishing boats go
Collect their fill,
A wave washes
Away all the krill.
People who live by
The seashore
Hear a deafening roar,
Everybody thinks
She wants to hurt us, but
We're the ones
Who hurt her and
Her beloved ocean.

Genevieve Tanner-Stokes (9)
Meole Brace Church Of England Primary And Nursery, Shrewsbury

Golden Boot Winner

Where do I start?
The World Cup, Kylian Mbappé,
A hat-trick against Argentina.
What a volley from him, and the penalty,
Kylian Mbappé has moved to Real Madrid from PSG.
Mbappé has never won the Ballon d'Or
But he is already at Real Madrid.
He scored match by match,
He scored from the halfway line,
The fans fainted,
Win the treble with Bellingham and Vini Jr.

Eli Burgoyne (8)
Meole Brace Church Of England Primary And Nursery, Shrewsbury

Water Rift 2.0

The miner saw fire in a sign that said Top Hill,
People were patient for the ancient cave,
But all that the miner found was a jaw-dropping pit,
And a waterfied wire,
The pyroclastic miner swung across the water,
Did a 360 and mined and did find rubber already.
The diamond he saw was trapping him with rubber
And the portal sent him to season four...

Joseph Warren (9)
Meole Brace Church Of England Primary And Nursery, Shrewsbury

A Trip To Build-A-Bear

I went to Build-A-Bear,
To get a fluffy bear,
I chose to get a Hello Kitty,
Because I'm very picky.

I went to get the stuffing,
So I could get the clothing,
The clothing was very cute,
So, I went to get some boots.

We went to the till,
So we could pay the bill,
And I was so excited,
To make my toys united.

Maria Annunziata (8)
Meole Brace Church Of England Primary And Nursery, Shrewsbury

Guardians Of The Galaxy

O n top of the moon
U niverse is in front of you
T otal darkness everywhere

O uter space
F lashing stars

S parkling spaceships
P lanets in many different colours
A stronauts are flying
C onstellations are flying
E arth is behind us.

Harper Beatty (8)
Meole Brace Church Of England Primary And Nursery, Shrewsbury

Trick Or Treating Is The Best! (Read In A Scary Voice)

The moon is high, the wind is cold,
Knocking on the door, asking for a treat,
Pumpkins glow with eyes so bold,
Wearing slippers upon their feet.

With a treat in every hand,
Costumes bright and masks so strange,
It's Halloween and it's so grand,
The sweets you open as slow as a snail!

Ooh!

Izzy Kirby-Murray (8)
Meole Brace Church Of England Primary And Nursery, Shrewsbury

Wolf

A kennings poem

Pack hunter,
Deer killer,
Doom bringer,
Swift mover,
Clean killer,
Silent murderer,
Midnight stalker,
Forest dweller,
Brave animal,
Apex predator,
Moon howler,
Mouse chaser,
Ambush hunter,
Burrow digger,
Cave curler,
Hole sleeper,
Toss turner,
Deep sleeper.

Beatrix Doughty (8)
Meole Brace Church Of England Primary And Nursery, Shrewsbury

Football

F ootball is awesome,

O nly great and good,

O nly football can impress everyone,

T otally, you need to be strong,

B all is hard,

A wesome football is great for you,

L ovely football,

L egendary football is like cookies.

Sandaru Abeywickrama (8)

Meole Brace Church Of England Primary And Nursery, Shrewsbury

The Best Day Ever

I could see birds flying
Across the beautiful flowers on the ground.
I could see wonderful trees whooshing in the wind.
I could smell the lovely, gorgeous sky.
I could smell the calm, colourful plants.
I could taste the fabulous food.
I could taste the crunchy leaves.

Owen Cornwell (8)
Meole Brace Church Of England Primary And Nursery, Shrewsbury

Birthday

B est day yet,

I went to a water park,

R acing down the slide,

T hen splashing into the water,

H olding my water gun,

D ancing through the water,

A day to never end,

Y es, it was the best day ever.

Booker Pitas (8)

Meole Brace Church Of England Primary And Nursery, Shrewsbury

Buzzards

B uzzards are amazing
U p high in the sky
Z igging, zagging
Z igging, zagging here and there
A irborne like a jet
R ugby tackling animals
D angerous diving high
S oaring away in the distance.

Adrian Yomens (9)
Meole Brace Church Of England Primary And Nursery, Shrewsbury

Cooking

C arefully sprinkly brown sugar,
O btain the apples,
O pen the butter,
K eep it warm,
I n the oven, it's getting hotter,
N ow washing my hands, ready to eat,
G et a spoon for the good treat!

Dylan Harris (9)
Meole Brace Church Of England Primary And Nursery, Shrewsbury

Light And Dark

L ight is bright
I can see
G low in the dark
H igh in the sky
T ingling with might

D arkness
A ce of spades
R olling away, never fades
K eeping the stars at bay.

Mason Davies (8)
Meole Brace Church Of England Primary And Nursery, Shrewsbury

Horrible Halloween

I can see pumpkin faces,
Scary monsters,
Bony skeletons.

I can hear monsters
Growling.

I can taste my
Sweet treats.

I can smell candy.

I can feel the
Witch's cat's silky
Fur.

Logan Chidlow (9)
Meole Brace Church Of England Primary And Nursery, Shrewsbury

Steph Curry

S pectacular
T all
E nthralling
P oint guard
H appy

C ourageous
U npredictable
R apid
R uthless
Y elling, "Three-pointer!"

Conor Thomas (9)
Meole Brace Church Of England Primary And Nursery, Shrewsbury

Keep On Swimming

S wimming is good exercise,
W inning is fun,
I 'm amazing,
M oving like a flash,
M um thinks I'm great,
I never give up,
N ever stop,
G ive up never.

Aimee Cartwright (8)
Meole Brace Church Of England Primary And Nursery, Shrewsbury

The Super Shiba

S oft, fluffy thing came out of the bush.
H e was a cute, adorable shiba.
I t was as cute as a baby tiger.
B aby shiba. He was cute but clumsy.
A dorable shiba. He fell over a lot.

Oscar Rutherford (8)
Meole Brace Church Of England Primary And Nursery, Shrewsbury

Super Space

S hiny, sparkling stars,
P lanets in many colours,
A stronauts jumping to planets,
C ystals in the night and stars,
E arth spinning around the sun.

Lucy Butler (8)
Meole Brace Church Of England Primary And Nursery, Shrewsbury

Haunted House!

Frightening monster,
Creepy coffin,
Immense vase,
Strange painting,
Colossal bed,
Old knight,
Disturbing photo,
Dirty grave,
Scary bones!

Alba Evans (8)
Meole Brace Church Of England Primary And Nursery, Shrewsbury

Space Adventure

S mells like rotten eggs,
P eople think it smells nice,
A big, white circle,
C ould be as bright,
E arth behind us.

Lottie Dee (8)
Meole Brace Church Of England Primary And Nursery, Shrewsbury

Slime

S limy, stretchy slime
L ovely to play with,
I love it!
M agical slime,
E very day to play with.

Lily Evans (8)
Meole Brace Church Of England Primary And Nursery, Shrewsbury

The Flying Island

On a rainy day, a girl with an umbrella was going to her house. At the house, she took a shower because she was wet.

After the shower, she ate an apple and bread with cheese.

She went out the house, now she was going to the supermarket. There was no food at her house, it was a bit sad. When she was going to the supermarket, she saw a gigantic island in the sky! Tatata said, "OMG!" She was about to fly. She started flying, then she said, "*Someone, help!*"

When she was at the island, she said, "This is a dream!" but it was not! She had found a little boy, then the girl asked him, "What are you doing here?"

Then the boy said, "I just started flying and I just went here!"

The boy and the girl started getting in a panic, then the girl said, "We are going out, I promise you!"

"Okay."

The only thing that they found was an apple. She ate it and it was a normal apple. The island was breaking in the middle.

The island broke and they went out!

Lucas Tartari Franceschini (10)
Portway Junior School, Allestree

Me And The Tree

One day, I was walking in the breeze
When I noticed a laughing tree
The sun was shining, my friend was crying
All these emotions in a day
All I wanted to do was just play
The next day when I saw the tree
When I saw it I wanted to flee
It was smiling this time
The sun started to shine
It started to rain, then I felt the pain
The pain of being alone, on this day
My friend then shouted, "Hey!"
A rainbow appeared, then disappeared
I don't know what happened
It was like an apple falling from a tree
It was mysterious, like my mum, Mrs Lyrious
The next day, I came again
All I wanted to do was play again
The tree was very happy to see me
So I started to flee
But when I was running
I felt so cunning
So, I went back to the sack by the tree

It was full of lemons
Then, I saw a boy called Jennons.

Imogen Marriott
Portway Junior School, Allestree

The Seasons

These are the seasons changing fast
This is spring here at last
Leaves regrow into something pink
This is the season when you clean your sink
Now warmth comes wandering in
It appears the sun begins to win
These are the seasons changing fast
This is summer here at last
Leaves turn into something more green and pretty
People prepared to leave this city
To go to the beach
But I'm afraid this heat
Is changing
These are the seasons changing fast
This is autumn here at last
Leaves turn orange and gather on a wall
This is the season some call fall
These are the seasons changing fast
This is winter
A season with jolly Christmas spirits and New Year's joy
This is winter and it's still not past.

Robyn Stevenson
Portway Junior School, Allestree

Summertime And Autumn

I love being in the big bright sun
When I'm beneath, I have such fun
When I head for the sun, I always bring
My super lucky magic ring
It brings me luck wherever I go
It works in any weather, sun, rain and snow
I think the sun is the very best thing
I tell my sister the sun can sing
And when she asks why it isn't right now
I just ignore her and talk to my friend
'Cause when she asks a question
The questions never end
There goes summer, quick as a flash
Next it's autumn, say goodbye to the past
We have such fun kicking the leaves
We spell out words, words like 'believe'.

Agnes Crowley (9)
Portway Junior School, Allestree

Outer Space Feline

You look up with your giant magic eye,
Staring longingly at the sky,
Little did you know, above the clouds and snow,
Is a little cat on a nebula,
Looking at your world.

She stares sadly at the constellation Orion,
Looks at all the satellites flyin',
For there's only one of her,
No other cats grooming fur.
There once was.

She stares at Earth,
Now she's mad
With a hint of sad,
Due to humans, they all died!
A grudge that'll never lie.

Nora Watkinson (8)
Portway Junior School, Allestree

The Autumn Tree

The mighty tree stands tall, no matter what the
weather,
Through summer, winter, autumn and spring,
It stands tall, even when it loses its leaves,
The mighty tree stands tall.

It likes people coming to see it,
The people like the tree, they come no matter what the
weather,
Through summer, winter, autumn and spring,
They sit on the bench next to the tree,
They climb and sit on it,
The mighty tree stands tall.

Finn Waldron (9)
Portway Junior School, Allestree

The Rainbow Friends

As you collect the lightbulbs
As you hide in a box
As you steal from Purple's lair
As you go on Orange's cavern coaster
As you run from Cyan, Green, Blue and Purple
When you go on the irrelevant trip to the odd world
Blood beyond happiness
Red creates as you go from birth to death
But you win from time to time
When you go on the rainbow friend roller coaster run
Suddenly, Cyan chases you.

Phoenix Morgan (9)
Portway Junior School, Allestree

Vegetables

My broccoli won't come back!
I'll have to catch it in a sack!
Pointless peas on the run.
While carrots blaze in the sun.
Missing potatoes brown and black.
Sundried tomatoes in the back of the sack.
Sweetcorn running through the fields.
Lettuce rocking high heels!
Forgot my tomatoes running away.
Now the potatoes start to sway.
Cabbages in rollerskates.
Rolling beside a landscape.

Connie Newboult (9)
Portway Junior School, Allestree

School Lunch

It's lunchtime, and I'm at school lunch
Barf! So, the reason I hate school lunch is because the
dinner ladies are awful
They should be in The World's Worst Teachers book
The reason they are so awful is because
They make the worst food
Today was pizza day
I know what you're thinking - you get pizza!
But the toppings are awful
They put bugs and leaves on it. It's awful.

Ella Kelsall (9)
Portway Junior School, Allestree

Animal Wonder

I wonder why
A chicken can't fly
But a seagull can do all three
Like walk and fly and swim
Unlike you and me

I wonder why
A cheetah is so fast
And always makes
The tortoise last
But if the cheetah should fall asleep
The tortoise might make it
Through snow and sleet!

Keziah Beatham (9)
Portway Junior School, Allestree

Another Day In Space...

There are scary things in space like TON 618,
Stephenson 2-18,
Phoenix A
And nebulae
But there is one thing more creepy and twisted
It killed all life on Uranus
4.3 billion years ago.
If you hear its blood-curdling screams
Run and hide
It's going to take over or kill Earth!

Isabelle Walker (10)
Portway Junior School, Allestree

Amazing Animals

Animals are amazing!
I don't get why we kill them.
We should be kind to all living beings,
Even if there are some downsides (meaning even if the
poo smells).
Please take in this note but be careful not to take in
the smell!
But really please do stop!
What did they do to you?

Emmy Gardner (9)
Portway Junior School, Allestree

Autumn

Autumn is September, October and November.
Autumn is full of orange, red, yellow and brown.

A nimals
U nder the
T rees
U ntil the
M onth is
N othing.

Brenee (10)
Portway Junior School, Allestree

Fish!

A big blue pond next to a brown village
Fishes of all sorts live
Always good except for the big bad fish
They kill with red in the good blue sea
Turned to blood-red
Like a beautiful rose.

Ebony Carmichael (9)
Portway Junior School, Allestree

I Wish I Could Go Back

I wish I could go back
To when I was read bedtime stories
About princesses and beasts,
Cuddled by a warm blanket
In the night, while the stars shone bright.
Now the stars just sit there,
And the storybooks are catching dust, away
As I stare blankly at the ceiling.

I wish I could go back
To when I wrote stories about
Radiant rainbows and fluffy clouds
Clouds like pillows in the sky
A flying bird, I was
Soaring ever so gracefully
Until my wings stopped working, broken.
Shattered. Useless. Broken.

I wish I could go back
To when I wasn't mopping floors
Day and night - hour by hour
"Worth two nickels and a penny," they say
Each second my energy devoured
It was simple when it wasn't me

As I waited eagerly for my parents to come back home.
But now I'm the one coming back.

I wish I could go back
To when I looked in the mirror
And thought the reflection was my twin.
I named her Gwen, she was my twin.
Now I don't see her any more, I see
A past of me, hidden, covered under layers
Of pretend and masquerade.

Gwen left, I stayed.

Now I'll regret that moment for the rest of my days.

Pritisha Lahkar (10)
St Eanswythe's CE Primary School, Folkestone

Space

S o, it's about space,
P acing on the moon and stars,
A giant power like a mace,
C reation looks up to it,
E verything like a dream,

I t's helping me to think,
S topping to observe as a team,

W ow! It's amazing.
O ver and over, I look back,
N ever to go past without force,
D aydreaming about an alien attack,
E verything is now a blur,
R iding a moon car on the moon,
F un, fun like never before
U nderstanding: must come back soon,
L eaving space is very loud.

Vlad Lynnyk (10)
St Eanswythe's CE Primary School, Folkestone

Me And The Silence Of Space

Drifting around
Alone, alone
Just me and the silence of space

The planets are spinning
But not my head
Just me and the silence of space

I don't need to think
Or worry, be scared
Just me and the silence of space

Floating weightless, calm
Peaceful, serene
Just me and the silence of space

Just me and the silence of space.

Aurora Portnyagin (9)
St Eanswythe's CE Primary School, Folkestone

Celestial Symphony

S tars shimmer like diamonds in a velvet sea,
P lanets dance in cosmic symphony,
A steroids drift as whispers in the night,
C elestial orbs glow with a gentle light,
E ternity stretches as far as eyes can see.

Alexander Wilkes (10)
St Eanswythe's CE Primary School, Folkestone

The End Of Spring

A haiku

Cherry blossoms bloom,
Summer sun shines bright today,
Autumn, winter next.

Ruby Nice (10)

St Eanswythe's CE Primary School, Folkestone

Frogs

Slimy little creatures of the wild
With skin very smooth and mild
Some are poisonous, some are transparent
But most are just cute!
Don't get too close or else... *croak!*

You'll probably find them on a thick oak log
Or by a bog
You can have them as a pet
And take them to the vet!
They're very small
Shorter than a brick wall
Keep them in a tank
So they don't rob a bank!
Just kidding, they're too small to do that!

They have massive tongues
But very small lungs
They have big beady eyes
But they can't even knead bread
They can jump across trees!
Boing, boing, boing

I think we can all agree
That frogs are better than bees

But some people disagree!
Not all frogs are green
Which doesn't mean they're mean
They can be red, orange, blue, yellow, white, green and more
And I think that's more than enough to adore
So after all of this
Frogs are still number one in my heart.

Leo Charles (8)
St Michael's CE (A) First School, Penkridge

To Me

I wake up with exhilaration
And I can't wait to see my best friend!
Excited to get to school
Praying the day doesn't end.
The laughs, the gossip, the hugs and more...
When I'm with them, I'm literally rolling on the floor!
Growing up is a hard thing!
It makes me feel quite queasy
But with my friends around me
It's easy-peasy!

It can be hard getting older
And parents just don't understand the stress
But when I'm with my four besties
I couldn't care less.
When I can't hold my tears back
I know my friends have my back.
They don't understand what they mean to me.
Their time, their laughter, their friendship
It's timeless to me.
My friends...
Are out of this world to me.

Esmae Boreland (8)
St Michael's CE (A) First School, Penkridge

Autumn

Leaves falling gently off the tree,
Piling up in front of me.
Some are big, and some are small,
In America, it's called fall.
Some are brown, some are gold,
It's a pretty sight to behold.
Picking pumpkins, which one's the best,
Maybe dress it up in an orange vest.
Carving pumpkins, a witch or a fairy,
Maybe something really scary.
The fifth of November, a date to remember
When fireworks light up the sky,
Guy Fawkes attempted to blow up the Houses of
Parliament,
Little did he know he would die.
This is my favourite season,
We share something the same,
It's very special,
We share the same name.

Autumn.

Autumn Byrne (9)
St Michael's CE (A) First School, Penkridge

The Snow Leopard

Below the cliffs, on a misty night,
A *crunch* could be heard in the snow,
A snow leopard was prowling around the trees,
The big cat wasn't cold,
As she had her furry coat on,
However, her cosy coat was far too old,
And she cried out for a new one,
Then an ice fairy came and gave her a new coat,
Now all she needed was food to eat,
Not fruit or veg, but a slice of meat,
She pounced on a deer and gobbled a boar,
Then let out a huge *roar*,
Now, at last, it was time for sleep,
So off she went to count some sheep.

Elsie Shearwood (9)
St Michael's CE (A) First School, Penkridge

Climate Change

The temperature is going up,
If it continues we'll be out of luck.
Polar bears will become a myth,
Because the ice caps start to drip.

Orangutans will lose their homes,
Because we choose to cut down thrones.
Turtles' playgrounds are no longer fantastic,
Because it's filled with all our plastic.

Birds' travels are becoming harder,
Because humans are travelling further.
If we don't get a grip of the mess,
No amount of luck will stop our stress.

Jacoby Landsborough (8)
St Michael's CE (A) First School, Penkridge

Timothy's Bananas

There was a curious monkey,
His name was Timothy,
He lived in the top of a tree,
On his adventures, through the trees, he swung,
He had so much confidence for a monkey so young,
All through the day, the birds would sit there and chirp,
But after Timothy had a banana he would release a
loud burp!
With his wind, he took a tumble
And scared the other animals in the jungle,
As all the animals ran away free,
Timothy cheered, "That's more bananas for me!"

Deyan P (8)
St Michael's CE (A) First School, Penkridge

A Questionable Life

As soon as I opened my tiny eyes I was here.
A baby built with fear and a family for some comfort.
I could say I was an innocent toddler.

Now I can walk, I love my sister.
And talk now I'm in school.
I have a friend and a life.
Sometimes I don't know who I am.
And question why I'm here.
But I carry on.

Soon I am a teen.
I have a phone and a boyfriend.
I still love life as an adult.

Millie-Jane Ainsworth (9)
St Michael's CE (A) First School, Penkridge

Heroes Are Everyone

From the ground to the sky
Some heroes fly high
While some heroes walk on the ground
Others don't hear a sound
While some heroes can't see
Other heroes help like me
Heroes come in many different shapes and sizes
Who all deserve a lot of prizes
From fighting crime
To reading a bedtime story
There's no stronger superpower than love
Heroes are everyone.

Olivia Withington (8)
St Michael's CE (A) First School, Penkridge

Animals Are Amazing

A nimals are amazing.

N oses are wet and rubbery.

I n the mud, and looking cuddly.

M ixed-up colours, playful and fun.

A mongst the tall trees, they gallop and run.

L ooking for prey or sleeping all day.

S talking in the sandy savannah, they always find their way.

Ivy Armitage (8)
St Michael's CE (A) First School, Penkridge

Food

Food keeps us alive,
Food is delicious,
Food is important,
There is healthy and unhealthy food,
Hot dogs, pizza, and apples too.
Wraps and cats... Wait, that's not food!

Holly Wootton (9)
St Michael's CE (A) First School, Penkridge

My School Rules

"No running down the corridor!" my teacher screamed.
"No sleeping during lessons," the teacher gleamed.

I ran down the corridor, this wasn't great,
I slept whilst the teacher read, now I'm in a state!

"No shouting in the classroom," she growled.
"No electronics," she said, as we howled.

I hurt myself, *ow!*
My phone made noises. *Oh, not now.*

"No daydreaming in my classroom," she said
suspiciously.
"No eating," the teacher whispered viciously.

I got bored and started to daydream.
I was hungry and could not resist an ice cream.

I ran, I slept, I was hungry and what next?
I was staring into space, thinking what I should text.

"Argh!" my teacher went.
"This wasn't what I meant!"

There was one place for me, and that was the head
teacher's office.
"Sorry! I will behave next time, Mr Morris!"

Haadiya Saifullah (10)
St Silas CE Primary School, Blackburn

The Riddle Of The Starry Night

I twinkle and sparkle up in the sky,
But you can't ever touch me, no matter how high,
I'm bigger than mountains but tiny to see,
What am I, this riddle as wide as the sea?
I float around planets, I tug on the moon,
I dance with the sun, morning, night and noon.
I never make noise, yet I'm always around,
I'm the quietest secret, but oh so profound.
I shine without stopping, I never grow old,
I'm made up of stories that never get told.
You wish on my glimmer when you see me glow,
But what am I, this friend you don't even know?
I'll give you a hint if you're scratching your head,
I light up the darkness where dreams love to tread.

Yes, I am a star, high and bright in the sky,
And now that you've guessed me, let's wave a
goodbye!

Ummul Khair Jamil (7)
St Silas CE Primary School, Blackburn

Unknown

As tall as a giraffe, I am slender and graceful,
If we do cross paths, it will be eventful.

As strong as a bear,
I will never harm you, not even a strand of your
beautiful hair.

As proud as a peacock, I really don't care
About the opinions of others, neither here nor there.

As mysterious as the majestic tufted deer,
You will be intrigued to come near
And have absolutely nothing to fear.

As sly as a fox, I am truly cunning
And can convince you of anything.

As quiet as a mouse
You will never even know I am in your house.

As beautiful as the sun and as bright as the moonlit
sky,
What am I?

Anayah Ali (10)
St Silas CE Primary School, Blackburn

My Day

Work is over
Time for rest
It's finally here
I feel the best
I wrap up warm
Cover my chest
Pray to God
My dream is blessed
'Cause in my dreams
I feel so free
In my dreams
I can be me
I fly real high
I surf the sea
Can be what I choose to be
Befriend a giant
Fight a dragon
Steal a ship
Fire the cannon
Fly through space
At the spell of the light
I love my dreams
They last all night

I'll fall in love
Have three children
Watch them grow
Help and teach them
Show them right
Tell them wrong
I love my dreams
They last so long
And when I wake
I cannot wait
To finish work
My bed is great.

Hira Ashraf (8)
St Silas CE Primary School, Blackburn

What Are Emotions?

Autumn wonders, what are emotions?
So she reads a book about emotions and demotions,
First in the book was happy, joy
Like from a toy,
Second in the book was sadness,
I can't take it from her crying,
Third in the book was furious anger,
I'm sorry that I hung you on a hanger,
Fourth in the book was emerald disgust,
She wanted to suspiciously discuss,
And last, but not least, fearful fear,
Aah! There's a massive bear,
Autumn finally finished the book,
She checked her watch with a pretty good look,
In class was a boring test,
She got an A+ in her first fest,
After a while, she was reading the books again.

Eleora Onuyoh-Adaitire (8)
St Silas CE Primary School, Blackburn

Spring Blossom

S oftly they awaken, petals in the breeze
P ainting the world with colours that please
R adiant hues burst forth from the earth
I nviting joy, celebrating rebirth
N ature's canvas a vibrant display
G ifting us beauty, as winter gives away.

B ees hum a tune, dancing from bloom to bloom
L avish fragrances waft, dispelling the gloom
O pening hearts to the warmth of the season
S haring their splendour without hesitation
S pring blossoms whisper
O ffer up wonder
M agnolias, daffodils, tulips in line.

Ermina Lokhandwalu (10)
St Silas CE Primary School, Blackburn

I Feel Emotions

There are a lot of different emotions
There are too many to count
Joy, fear, anger, sadness
They are the main ones that come out!

They all work in a different way
Just like magic potions
Feeling joy makes you happy
Feeling anger makes you snappy

When you feel sad
Sometimes it can make you mad
And sometimes sadness can lead to fear
But just remember it doesn't always lead to a tear

You can always talk to a friend or family
Sometimes it can help
No matter how scary emotions are
Just know that you will always be a *star!*

Kiran Ilyas (8)
St Silas CE Primary School, Blackburn

Adventures

Walking alone in the jungle,
One day a lot of bushes were in my way,
Monkeys were climbing,
While I was dancing,
Birds were chirping,
While I was singing,
Rabbits were jumping above the grass,
As some weird animal passed,
Suddenly I heard a *roar*,
Or was it just a snore?
It was a tiger who stared,
I was badly scared,
As this was happening,
My eyes were opening,
My dad next to me was snoring!

Azwa Saifullah (8)
St Silas CE Primary School, Blackburn

Failures

It's okay to make
Mistakes
To fail and
To
Try again
Lots of
People
Can fail
Or make
Mistakes
Without them
We
Wouldn't
Be able
To learn from
People
And
Lift ourselves
Up!

Imaan Ahsan (10)
St Silas CE Primary School, Blackburn

Nature

N ature, oh what a thing!
A pleasant breeze flows through me.
T he sunflowers grow and the sun shines with glee.
U mbrellas? No need for them at all!
R eady for some summertime fun?
E verybody loves nature!

Khalifa Khalifa (9)
St Silas CE Primary School, Blackburn

Space Is Wonderful

S pace is a mystery
P laces are unknown
A universe never ends
C ome and explore space
E njoy the life of space.

Myiesha Umair (9)
St Silas CE Primary School, Blackburn

Go To Space

Goku goes to space
Everyone can live
No one can beat us.

Ali Dudhara (8)
St Silas CE Primary School, Blackburn

Scare At Midnight

S tranger on the streets

C reeping around, following us with each and every step

A m I scared? Definitely.

R unning for our lives, escaping the danger amidst this perilous person

E very corner is scarier in which we turn into, chills flow down my spine.

A step is one more further from home, please let this be a dream

T reating every step with caution and conscientiousness.

M aking a move, trying to throw this person off

I t is getting late, this figure won't stop but it will not stop me for sure

D ay turned to night, walking to swerving, and relaxed to anxiousness

N ot giving up easily, sprinting to catch us now. *Who are you? What do you want?*

I am exhausted trying not to give in, it's hopeless, but I continue

G etting rid of this situation was hard and inescapable but not impossible

H oping to get home soon, so I go to fight it off, suddenly I wake up.

T his was a dream, no, a nightmare, but it doesn't matter, I was safe in my bed, it was just my imagination, in a whirlwind, in my rested head on my pillow to dream away.

Harmony Whitehouse (10)
The Python Hill Academy, Rainworth

Time Flies...

Here I am in the beloved world,
My mother is happy because I am a girl,
Seeing my house for the first time,
It is so shiny, just like a dime.
Family happy to meet me,
I was so confused like a stinging bee,
My first ever one-year-old birthday,
I got a load of presents and cards today,
I bet you're surprised I can talk,
But this is all head in thought.
My sixth birthday I still could not talk,
It was very strange like scratching chalk,
I don't need a booster seat anymore!
But I need a safety liner, what a bore!
It was no fun today,
It was just a rainy day!
I am fourteen!
But why can I still not talk in my teens?
My first waterpark ride!
But that was last night...

Kacie Olivia Jepson (10)
The Python Hill Academy, Rainworth

Snow White

In a little cottage deep in the woods,
There was a young girl with lips red as blood,
Within the cottage were seven beds
To rest seven sleepy heads.

Dopey, Bashful, Sneezy, Sleepy, Happy, Grumpy, Doc
All fell asleep to the sound of a ticking clock.
When they woke, they were met with a shock,
For sitting there was their broken clock.

Georgia Cox (10)
The Python Hill Academy, Rainworth

Autumn Daze

When leaves start to fall
And people wear their woolly coats
Leaves turn from green to orange
All these things I love so well
Waiting for leaves to fall
To hear their crunch
Under our feet
Red, orange and gold
Maybe pumpkins are ready
Do not pick mushy ones
For deep inside are little bugs in their home
The time for scary decorations
And trick-or-treaters
Scary costumes all around
In the autumn daze
People wear their woolly hats
And little kids wear their mittens
To keep their hands warm
They begin to use the fireplace
Time for leaf art
And boots on your feet

Fog fills the air
Ready
For the autumn haze?

Macey Green (10)
The Python Hill Academy, Rainworth

Never Enough

I try and try but I still haven't tried hard enough
I work and work but I still haven't worked hard enough
I look and look but I still haven't looked far enough
This mountain is too tall, I will fall
You push and push, you've pushed hard enough
I have met my limit
I am only a child, don't let me fall.

Evie-May Lebeter (10)
The Python Hill Academy, Rainworth

Halloween

H ear the screams in the night
A ll around such a fright
L ights shining in your eyes
L ooking at you deep inside
O h so scary in the light
W aving left and right
E verywhere you look
E verything's been took
N ever knowing what's safe.

Skyla Pearce (10)
The Python Hill Academy, Rainworth

Autumn Days

The sky was an art piece, yellow and red
The sun was going down as it was sunset
Trees were like skyscrapers
Towering up high
Higher and higher and higher
Going up to the sky
Amber leaves pirouetted through the air above
Kids were sad as when summer ended, so did their summer fun.

Katelin Jane Ross (9)
The Python Hill Academy, Rainworth

Seasons Change Fast

Autumn leaves fly around in the sky,
Winter is close by,
Here comes winter with a cold breeze of ice,
Spring enters with a surprise,
Flowers blooming, bees buzzing,
Summer comes, moving with the sun,
Olympics come, people have won,
Then it repeats again and again.

Ruby-Mae White (10)
The Python Hill Academy, Rainworth

YoungWriters
Est 1991

Walk Through The Forest

F or once, my mum let me walk by myself.
O ver the river and through the trees.
R eindeer hopping about.
E very time I go through, I hear voices.
S un is setting, deer are going to bed.
T omorrow, we can do it all again.

Lily Hatcher (10)
The Python Hill Academy, Rainworth

Autumn

A pples falling off the trees,
U sually gets cooler from the breeze,
T ime for raking up those leaves,
U nderneath the stars in the sky,
M oments like these, I'm on a high,
N ights pass by in the blink of an eye.

Evie Dakin (10)
The Python Hill Academy, Rainworth

Otters

O tters all over the world
T imed in a swirl
T ickles their tummy
E verything is funny
R ivers flowing
S ome fishermen rowing.

Abigail Newey (11)
The Python Hill Academy, Rainworth

If I Had Wings

If I had wings I would dance in the rain
Float in the air
And fall through the clouds
No one would stop me
As they would have too much pleasure watching me
I would visit the gods and goddesses
I would fight in the war
Save lives from fire
I would get to school on time
I might even be the most popular
Everyone would shower me with gifts
The wings on my back
Would create rainbows
My life would be perfect
I could drift to the moon
Even the sun wouldn't stop me
The only thing in control
Would be my imagination
That's when I wake up
My dad's in my room
It was all a real dream
My dream.

Kara Prideaux-Brune (10)
Truro High School For Girls, Truro

The Dance In The Dark

At the night of the grand ball,
Something seemed to go astray,
The costume was ready,
The stage was set,
But something went wrong, I bet,
As the girl mounted the stage,
She knew this was an important day,

The red curtain parted,
She danced and she twirled,
But who let the rope slip?
Who would want to hurt a little girl?
It fell from the sky,
Smashing all the lights,
Landing backstage, giving everyone a fright,
And there at night,
Looking serene and smart,
She performed the dance in the dark.

Agnes Watkins (9)
Truro High School For Girls, Truro

The Magic Dog

Mum ran through the door, *splat!*
Some magic on the floor
A splat of this and a splog of that
But especially upon the dog

Our dog turned magic straight away
And went outside to play
Where it grew two huge ears
"Oh look!" cried Mum, pointing down low
I didn't know our dog had huge ears

Then with a flick of Tiddles' ear
She turned Mum into a grasshopper
Me into a snail
And Dad into a slug

Then Tiddles
Took over
The house!

Ashleigh Balsdon (10)
Truro High School For Girls, Truro

Henry Tudor

H e is cruel but crucial
E ats ten times more than you
N ever keeps the same wife
R egal instructor of head choppings
Y ou never want to meet brutal Henry the Eighth.

T otally ridiculous and definitely unfair
U tterly smart and positively disgraceful
D ungeons are home for you if you break one rule
O ver ten times wider than you
R eally I'm telling you never meet Henry the Eighth.

Cecilia Srikanthan (9)
Truro High School For Girls, Truro

The Wild Zoo

Wobbly wombat waddled in his cage,
Trying tiger scared the teenagers,
Striking sausage dog barked at the elegant elephant,
Elegant elephant got scared by the striking sausage dog,
Brown bear grizzled at the customers,
Curious cat came over and scratched the worker,
Magical meerkat disappeared,
Active axolotl swam all around his tank,
Rapid rabbit hopped around the zoo,
Beautiful butterfly fluttered in the clucking chicken's face.

Annabelle Cave (9)
Truro High School For Girls, Truro

Butterflies

B eautiful butterflies soaring in the sky
U p they fly so very high
T errific they are with colours so light
T iny they are but brave and bright
E very spring they fly up high
R are they are in the winter trees
F inally, they're free from their cocoons
L ovely wings with patterns and marks
Y ou and me, we butterflies fly up high and land down low.

Olivia Chapman (10)

Truro High School For Girls, Truro

Football

F or I am football frenzy

O h footballers if you see

O nly the best team win the cup

T he love for football is very strong

B ringing myself to my feet I shout, "Hooray!" when they score a goal

A iming for the goal, there's a shiver up my spine

L ining up to give fist bumps to the other team

L oving football is my thing and always will be.

Charlotte Fox (9)
Truro High School For Girls, Truro

Crocodile

C ruel, amphibious monster
R uling the lake in which he lurks
O n the river bank, lazily snoring
C homper who skulks in the marshlands
O ver in the swamp, that's where he romps
D readed fish eater
I n the mud, out of sight
L ow down, ready to strike
E lated when he spots prey.

Matilda Soar (9)
Truro High School For Girls, Truro

Grey Wolves

G raceful and deadly,
R azor-sharp claws as white as the moon,
E yes as yellow as gold,
Y ou need to be cautious around these animals,

W olves are as scary as any animal should be,
O ver the forest they roam,
L oving mothers to adorable cubs,
F avourite for some, deadly for most.

Georgie Hose (9)
Truro High School For Girls, Truro

What If

What if you could fly high in the sky?
You would be a true hero!

What if you didn't go to school?
What would you do?

What if everything was for free?
Life would be a dream.

What if everyone's hair was 50m?
Good luck washing it!

What if life had no questions?
I wonder.

Sienna Hensher (9)
Truro High School For Girls, Truro

Dreams And Nightmares

My nightmares carry burning sombreness to my
thoughts
My dreams lift magical light that showers the
morning's night
When they unite, the stars shine
Like the cold winter sky
Nightmares always win
But never fear
The light is always near
Just look around the corner in your dreams.

Dora Galsworthy (9)
Truro High School For Girls, Truro

Riddle Me!

I rise, tall and proud,
I'm towering above the muddy ground,
I can be a mellow, yellow and chestnut brown!
I'm in no way a stupendous, ferocious beast,
Don't worry, I'm a herbivore, you're not my feast!
Unlike my other friends, I am free,
I'm an elegant giraffe, can't you see?

Beany Sautelle-Smith (9)

Truro High School For Girls, Truro

The Fright Of Halloween

On Halloween, it's dark as night,
And to many people, it gives such a fright.
They dress up in costumes of unspeakable things as they walk around the streets,
And all the little children go knocking on doors, hoping for tasty treats.
I know this sounds a little crazy, but Halloween still scares me!

Indie Singer (10)
Truro High School For Girls, Truro

What Am I?

I strike at the dead of night.
I have snowy white fur.
My signature noise sends shivers down your spine.
My claws are as sharp as needles.
I have amber eyes.
Proud and sturdy, I stalk my prey,
My teeth are as sharp as knives,
Running wild, I chase my prey.
I am an Arctic wolf.

Florence Floyd (9)
Truro High School For Girls, Truro

Football Fantasy

Haiku poetry

Avid players strive,
Under my malicious eye,
The Champions League.

Sleep-depriving games,
For every player aims,
The Champions League.

Gems of new players,
Such a good generation,
The Champions League.

A few thousand clubs,
Some fighting relegation,
The Champions League.

Nia Burnard (9)
Truro High School For Girls, Truro

What Am I?

To my prey, I am green with black stripes.
To human eyes, I am orange with black stripes.
I strip off meat to eat.
I have fangs as sharp as steel.
I am endangered in my habitat. Please help me.
What am I?

Answer: Yes, I am a tiger!

Grace Hamilton (9)

Truro High School For Girls, Truro

The Wolfhound Forest

You can hear wolfhounds howling at the moonlight
You can see ocean-green ivy crawling up the barky trees
You can feel silky green ferns in the gloomy forest
You can see a tiger trying to pounce to the other side of the mossy river.

Lula Myers (9)
Truro High School For Girls, Truro

Totoro

T rees he grows,
O ak fruits are what he feasts on,
T errific tree spirit he may be,
O val is his shape,
R oars for the Catbus,
O ccasionally, he uses his magical flute.

Flo Latham (9)

Truro High School For Girls, Truro

Halloween

H ail

A ll dead souls

L ong-lost and

L oved ones

O nly tonight

W e welcome you back

E nchanted evening

E nding summer

N earing fall.

Lily Eustice (9)
Truro High School For Girls, Truro

I Am Your Nightmare

I'm lurking in the shadows
Bloodthirsty
Red watering eyes
Burning fire
Sparkling teeth
Deadly dragon claws
Deep snorting nostrils
Smoking flames flying around.

Maisie Green (9)
Truro High School For Girls, Truro

Winter With Me

Winter, like every snowflake, it's different everywhere.
Winter, hot chocolate with my dog and the tear of
wrapping paper.
Presents being unveiled, unwrapped.
Uncle Jim got me a jam jar,
Aunty Jill gave me a thrill when I opened a present to
find a puppy and a guppy!
Winter is walking out in what feels like a thousand
layers
Just to take most of them off as soon as you get hot.
Winter is snowball fights
And watching the snowmen sway in the early morning
breeze.
The lights that light up the streets with illuminations,
Glimmers that shine on the curb.
Snow is like an arrow has burst a giant balloon.
Snow, it feels like a battalion of parachuting soldiers
falling from the misty sky.

Rafe Mitchell (10)
Woodcote House School, Windlesham

Detention!

"Class, pay attention, or else get a detention!"
But how could I concentrate when my dog ate my homework?
No one would believe me that my dog ate it,
His annoying little smirk across his greedy face.
"Get out your homework, everyone!"
"I don't have my homework, sir."
"Detention then!"
Detention is a prison people never leave.

I heard of a boy called Ned who never came out of detention.
"Attention, everyone in detention!"
Did you mention detention?
To Mr Dee with tension?
Time stops in detention
Call the cops in detention
Mr O in detention
D.E.T.E.N.T.I.O.N.
What does that spell?
Detention!

Charlie Brittain (11)
Woodcote House School, Windlesham

Joy For Glizzys

Amazing glizzy, so scrumptious.
I've never tasted anything so delicious.
One glizzy, two glizzys, three glizzys.
Three great glizzys, straight down the pipe.
My mangos were quite ripe.
They were nice and watery.
Chomp! Glizzys are as tasty as a creamy doughnut.
I waddled back with a stomach of glizzys, to my hut.

My eyes were glittering stars as I looked in the mirror.
The red sausage shined in its reflection.
They feel like magic all around.
Then came the hound.
It came bounding in.
Took the glizzy right out of my hand.
When It came to land
I snatched it right back
And slid it down my throat.
They are my favourite roti.

Kevin Liu (10)
Woodcote House School, Windlesham

Don't Be Mean

Meanness is something wrong to do
It is bullying, it can hurt someone or even kill someone
There was a big bully called Charlie
He would always hit other children
We called him the Notorious Killer, Big Charlie or
speaking of the devil
I'm scared of Big Charlie
I'm scared of the Notorious Killer
I'm scared of the devil
All of the kids told the principal
Then Big Charlie made his hand into a fist and hit the
principal
We were scared so we took a brush and hit Big Charlie
He went down and everyone was happy
Suddenly, Big Charlie hit me and boy did it hurt
I went down and that was how I got a scar.

Daniel Bore (11)
Woodcote House School, Windlesham

The School Bully

The school bully bullied me at games
His name's James
On the way home, he called me 'wimpy'
And kicked me and I became limpy.
At lunch while he threw food down his throat
He liked to lob food at the hob
At break he stayed at the fountain
Waiting for victims to tower over like a mountain
But one day his dad died
He went to hide
But I found him in the end
And he became my friend
So we put this all behind us
When we went on the school bus
And so James is my friend
To the very end.

Henry Stephenson (10)
Woodcote House School, Windlesham

Sun

In the morning, slowly rising from his bed,
The sun stretches his hands out and warms the land,
And wakes up the people to come out to work and
play.

At noon, the sun puts on his dark glasses,
And smothers sun cream on his face,
To cool down he hides behind the fluffy clouds,
He longs for the rain so that when it stops,
He can paint the sky in many colours.

He puts on one more show before going to bed,
He slowly closes his eyes and says, "Goodbye."
To the moon as she wakes up.

Hans Matharu (10)
Woodcote House School, Windlesham

The Ground, Air And Water

On the ground, the elephants stomp,
On the ground, there's a swamp.
In the air, the birds fly,
In the air, the sun is shy.
In the water, the dolphins play,
In the water, you could find some clay.
In the water, the whales dance,
On the ground, the horses prance.
In the air, the planes fly,
On the ground, the fries fry.
On the ground, people walk,
In the ground, you'll find some chalk.

Inigo Worth (11)
Woodcote House School, Windlesham

Chocolate

Chocolate, chocolate tastes so sweet,
It's such a creamy treat!
Chocolate, chocolate tastes so sweet,
It's my favourite treat!
Creamy, smooth, melts just right
A little bite is a big delight!
Milk or dark or in a bar
Chocolate is the best by far
Drizzled on cupcakes or in a cup,
It lifts me miles up when I feel stuck
Crunchy or soft, gooey inside
It makes me feel like I can fly.

Herbie Martin (10)
Woodcote House School, Windlesham

The Dogs

D ogs dash through the fields, they run so fast, like a blur of fur they never come last!

O utstretched paws leap high in the sky, they have never gone up, up so high.

G entle eyes gleam with care, always with me everywhere.

S oft, silky fur like a cosy rug, for every wag, we share a nice hug.

Alex Chase (10)
Woodcote House School, Windlesham

Winter Night

I slowly stroll down the path,
My face in the freezing breeze,
The whistling wind blowing my silky scarf,
My hands about to freeze.

There's snow in my boot,
There's nothing in sight,
This place must be mute,
As it's such a silent night.

Ralph Gutu (11)
Woodcote House School, Windlesham

Animals Of Africa

Rhinos running freely on the African plains
Among the zebras and giraffes grazing side by side
Wary of the lions and hyenas circling them
Looking for their lunch.
Leaping leopards in the trees
Climbing monkeys chasing each other.

Casper Wyke (10)
Woodcote House School, Windlesham

The Lion Cloud

The lion cloud ran,
We thought it was making a plan,
It came closer each day,
In each and every way.

The lion cloud ran,
We blew the lion cloud away,
With a massive fan,
During the month of May.

The lion cloud ran,
Far, far away.

Jonny Palmer (10)
Woodcote House School, Windlesham

My Family

When I am with my family, I am happy
When I see my grandfather, he takes me to the beach
We ride the waves and surf so high
Making big sandcastles under the sky
When I am with my family, I am happy.

Jaime Venero Loyo (10)
Woodcote House School, Windlesham

YOUNG WRITERS INFORMATION

We hope you have enjoyed reading this book – and that you will continue to in the coming years.

If you're the parent or family member of an enthusiastic poet or story writer, do visit our website **www.youngwriters.co.uk/subscribe** and sign up to receive news, competitions, writing challenges and tips, activities and much, much more! There's lots to keep budding writers motivated!

If you would like to order further copies of this book, or any of our other titles, then please give us a call or order via your online account.

Young Writers
Remus House
Coltsfoot Drive
Peterborough
PE2 9BF
(01733) 890066
info@youngwriters.co.uk

Join in the conversation!
Tips, news, giveaways and much more!

YoungWritersUK   **YoungWritersCW**

youngwriterscw   **youngwriterscw**